~may you
be happy~

Sara Jenkins

This Side of Nirvana

This Side of Nirvana

SARA JENKINS

FAIR WINDS
PRESS

GLOUCESTER, MASSACHUSETTS

Text © Sara Jenkins

First published in the USA in 2001 by
Fair Winds Press
33 Commercial Street
Gloucester, MA 01930

10 9 8 7 6 5 4 3 2 1

Printed and bound in the United States

Cover design by Kathryn Sky-Peck
Book design by Jill Feron/Feron Design

ISBN 1-931412-73-1

Excerpts are quoted from:

Songs of Kabir, translated by Rabindranath Tagore.
Macmillan Co., New York, 1915.

The Sign of Jonas. Thomas Merton.
Harcourt Brace and Co. New York, 1953.

Nirvana: . . . BLISS, HEAVEN; a goal hoped for but apparently unattainable.

Webster's Tenth Collegiate Dictionary

Contents

PREFATORY NOTE

The places mentioned in this book are real places, and the teachers are real teachers. The other people are real too, but their names have been changed; sometimes they are blends of several people, and often time and place have been compressed in the interest of succinctness. This story is simply the gist of what happened, from my point of view. What I hope to show are some of the remarkable benefits of Buddhist meditation practice for those of us who are something less than spiritual superstars.

My use of quotation marks reflects how the incidents described exist in my memory. That is, I "hear" people saying the things I have written, which is not to claim that those very words were spoken. Indeed, the spiritual path portrayed here calls into question most of what we think we know. My aim is to express the deeper truth of what I have learned as best as I can from where I am in the ever-changing understanding of life on this side of nirvana.

INTRODUCTION

For as far back as I can remember, I believed that I needed to do something to improve my life. I was most attracted to programs of my own devising, which at their best were vague and at their worst a bit grandiose: abandoning all else for true love, abandoning all else for a Cause. Methods urged by others—eat right and exercise, relax, smile—came in for consideration as well, and some of my plans, such as observing a day of rest, shared features with one or another spiritual paths. Once, having read about the benefits of concentrating on one's respiration, the only physiological function that is both voluntary and involuntary, I resolved to be aware of my breathing for the rest of my life. Occasionally, I imagined an alternative to imposing on myself any discipline at all, believing, however briefly, that happiness surely would be found in doing whatever I wanted to do.

One after another, life-improvement programs rose on the horizon, and I never quite noticed the point at which each evaporated somewhere overhead. But since I couldn't face my subsequent anxiety, I would quickly cast around for the next idea on how to make everything better. Eventually the exquisite hopefulness that attended each new beginning grew dull with repetition, and I feared I would never figure out what it was I should be doing, much less do it.

In retrospect I can see that there was nothing terribly wrong with my life, but that's not how it felt then. I had prolonged well into my thirties a restlessness that suits late adolescence but palls in its second decade, then grows urgent and embarrassing. My first fifteen years of adulthood were scattered among six universities, a dozen cities, and several countries, with a romance for each new place, along with assorted jobs and periods of dropping out to do some serious wondering about what it all meant. The idea of settling down crossed my mind now and then, but I could not decide what to settle down to, or with, or where, or why.

I can now see one dissatisfaction that may have helped propel me into spiritual practice, and that was that I had ended up teaching art history. Liking art is one thing, but teaching the history of it, I found, is quite another. One day during the last term that I taught, standing in the darkened room beside a slide projection of Rembrandt's *Three Trees*, I suddenly became unable to speak. My silence probably lasted only a few seconds, but because it was involuntary, it disturbed me, and I entertained dire thoughts about my mental health. Looking back, I see that incident in a different light. It was as if a firm but kindly hand gripped me, and held me still, so I could see the truth: I loved presenting those glowing images for people to admire, but I did not like trying to explain art.

After I left academic life and began to practice meditation, I noticed two interesting developments in myself. First, my tendency to define beauty ever more narrowly was reversed, along with the concomitant need to reject things because they are not beautiful. Second, my interest shifted from talking about beauty to simply enjoying it.

Long before I knew much about meditation, I already considered it my best chance for learning how to live. Meditation promised balance, and, between the extremes of grasping and despair, a center in which to rest. Meditation might undo the deleterious effects of academic life—all that reading, writing, and talking about things of no consequence to most of humanity—and restore the natural abilities to live more fully in the world. Yes, I thought: meditation must be the answer. Inward and upward!

Having looked for answers in the most obvious places in my own culture, from the wisdom preserved in great books to the latest fashions in psychotherapy, with intermittent forays into hedonism, I was ready to look elsewhere. This book is an account of where I looked and what I found.

The last resort, for me, was Buddhism.

Fortunately, this path can be followed by anybody, even those of us who need remedial training in concentration or who, for whatever reasons, consider ourselves "spiritually challenged." Indeed, that is where the path begins: sitting still with a wandering, restless mind. Noticing and accepting all one's imperfections, again and again and yet again. Learning to love, in spite of everything.

Nor does the path require that we approach it with noble intentions. What I brought to my spiritual seeking was the one thing I had going for me all along, although it took time to recognize its importance—the sincerity of my simple wish to be happy.

❖ ❖ ❖

There was a time, during the 1970s, when, like many of my friends, I conducted a short search for happiness amid the exotica of Asian religions—cruising the aisles, as they say, of the spiritual supermarket. I had started with the Yellow Pages, where I was pleased to find several listings under "meditation instruction." But yoga at the Y sounded too ordinary, Theosophy too heady, and the International Society for Krishna Consciousness too extreme.

When I read in *New York* magazine that artists, literati, intelligentsia, and the like were flocking to a swami installed in a Catskills resort for the summer, I decided to go too.

Joining such illustrious company seemed a safe way to take a look at the spiritual scene, and I might even learn meditation while I was at it.

The four-day "intensive" I attended had what I took to be the earmarks of true religion: chanting in a nonvernacular language (Sanskrit), holy smells (incense and sprinklings with rose water), portents of the miraculous (people in trance states), and the breathtaking sense of being in the presence of a saint. I had never given a thought to what "saint" meant, but somehow I knew that this little brown swami in a saffron robe and a knit ski cap was it.

After the intensive, I collected pictures of the swami, from flimsy patches of newsprint to glossy promotional photographs. (The latter were on sale in impressive variety at the swami's local meditation center, suggesting that mine was not a singular obsession.) Even though I taught medieval art history, I had never taken seriously the concept of sacred images, and the reverence I felt toward my motley trove—swami in a sweater and sunglasses, swami meditating in a loincloth, swami smiling from a large color portrait into the depths of my being—was deeply surprising to me. My feelings for the swami were a lot like being in love, with the added frisson of spiritual desire. Learning to meditate got lost in a swirl of longing and sweetness and awe.

When my ardor faded a few months later, my search resumed. I enrolled in a twelve-week meditation course sponsored by a Jewish-Christian group. No bells, no smells, no miracles, no saints, certainly no swamis. The group was led by a couple of psychologists, if I remember right, whose approach struck me as typically American in its businesslike tone. Each week we were introduced to a different form of meditation. For half an hour, we practiced counting our breaths or chanting or silently repeating a sacred mantra or visualizing a sacred image or looking at our reflections in a mirror and thinking of death. After the thirty minutes, we discussed what we had experienced. At the time, this practice seemed perfectly sensible, but in retrospect it has taken on a comical aura—the rapid transit approach to spiritual practice.

For me, that approach not only didn't work, but it also seemed to generate in me out-and-out negativity. I developed an acute case of what I suppose was unconscious resistance. From the second week on, after five or ten excruciating minutes of silence, I would be seized by a coughing attack. I would rise from my place in the circle of meditators, tiptoe out of the room, and slink wretchedly down the hall to the restroom, where my lungs contracted and heaved until my ribs ached and tears poured down my face. Then I would creep back again and take my place for the last few minutes of silence, after which the others reported blissful states in which hearts filled with love and all became One. My own heart, over the weeks, rankled with resentment and envy and shame.

Finally, I quit, unable to let go the tormenting thought that the experience had cost me eighty-five dollars. I made other efforts: a women's yoga class that met in a church, tai chi in the park, a discussion group on goddess traditions, feminist Episcopalianism. None of them seemed right for me, or I wasn't right for them.

When I went to India, then, at the end of the 1970s, it was not with any spiritual purpose. Intending merely to look at Buddhist and Hindu monuments for a course I taught on religious art, I gave wide berth to ashrams and swamis. All that was finished, I thought. My interest in spiritual matters was probably no more than a "phase" I was going through.

And yet the three books I carried with me were undeniably spiritual companions. Two were mystical poetry, by the Indian poets Kabir and Tagore. The third was a scholarly book on Tibetan Buddhism, which conveyed to me, somewhere between the Sanskrit and the footnotes, the insistent message

that the most important thing in my life was to learn to meditate—and that meditation was impossibly difficult. To make
up for my failings in that area, I committed to memory verses
of Kabir.

> Between the poles of the conscious and the unconscious,
>   there has the mind made a swing;
> Thereon hang all beings and all worlds, and that swing
>   never ceases its sway.

At about the midpoint in my travels, I ended up in a tiny
town in the middle of India. Sanchi is the site of three famous
Buddhist stupas, ancient masonry mounds representing,
through their original purpose as burial places, release from
suffering.

By the time I got there, I experienced a certain confusion
of purpose. I was indeed collecting material for my course, but
something else was going on as well. I could not wholly convince myself, for example, that it was purely for economic reasons that I did not stay at the obvious place, the Travellers'
Lodge, but chose instead a guest house connected with a small
Buddhist temple and monastery. And I had no explanation for
why I stayed day after day after day, when all I needed was a
few hours.

❖ ❖ ❖

Even with the benefit of hindsight, I recall nothing about my
arrival in Sanchi that could be construed as an auspicious sign
or portent. I was the only passenger who got off the train
there, and foremost in my awareness was the fact that in the
several months I had been traveling, Sanchi was the farthest I
had been from Western amenities and from other tourists.

The railway station and a scattering of nondescript structures did not add up to the kind of impression that even a small town would want to make on a visitor. For a moment, I considered climbing back onto the train, slipping into a window seat, and watching the next half of India go by, on my way to a coast, a city, civilization—anywhere but this place that looked like nothing.

A tiny, shriveled porter took my bags. I said I would need a rickshaw. No rickshaw, he said. A taxi then. No taxi. I told him I was going to the Mahabodhi Society. He waggled his head and led me out of the station. My destination, it turned out, was only a few steps down the dusty road. A series of sheds and stalls housing vendors and open-air eating establishments, the village version of a commercial strip, ended at a crossroads. To the right I could see the Travellers' Lodge, to the left a small museum. Beyond, there rose a hill crowned with the silhouette of one of the Buddhist stupas. Everything Sanchi had to offer was right there.

The porter left me at the heavy iron gates to the monastery compound. They were slightly ajar, so I went in. I found myself face-to-face with three monks. They almost seemed to be waiting for me, all smiles and bows. The head monk, who spoke some English, delivered a welcoming speech then led me to the guest quarters. In the small, sunny courtyard surrounded by flaking yellow walls, we stood for a few moments and exchanged more smiles. Then the monk pointed out my room and left.

The room was convent-clean and furnished with a cot and two folding chairs. On the cot was a pallet of rough, faded sacking, stuffed with some very natural fibers, smelling and feeling like a mixture of straw and Spanish moss. An adjoining room contained a private bath, consisting of a cold-water tap at about knee height and a squat toilet. I lay down on the cot, inordinately pleased to be in such simple and lovely surroundings. In the doorway, a handwoven curtain, embroidered with little temples, drifted back and forth in the breeze, admitting air and light and glimpses of bright straggly flowers outside.

For several days, I was the only guest. Each morning I made my way up ancient paths through groves of guava and ficus trees and gray-green briar bushes and banks of flowering lantana to the hilltop, where I spent timeless hours alone in the presence of the three sacred mounds. The stupas, symbolizing the mythic World Mountain, are solemn hemispheres of stone, brick, and stucco, encircled by walkways leading, spiritually speaking, inward and upward. The sculptural reliefs surrounding them, on the other hand, show an energetic jumble of earthly images: elephants, monkeys, birds, stylized trees, crowds of people, and emblems of the Buddha. There was a lot to look at.

On the first day, however, after making the ritual walk around each stupa, guidebook in hand, I decided that enough was enough. The rest of the time I spent on the hilltop simply enjoying the breeze, the solitude, and the vistas across green fields dotted with date palms and the soft, still Indian plain, its horizon muted in mist. Often I lay on my back on an old stone wall along the far rim of the hill, doing nothing. Day after day.

Occasionally I contemplated the stupas. I knew what the art history books said—that they were mythic symbols of the release from suffering. But what exactly did that mean?

I sensed that those days in Sanchi marked some change in me, but I thought of it in terms of my responses to external events. First, my wristwatch stopped running. I threw it away and easily learned to tell the hour by the sun. In Sanchi, I began washing my clothes by hand and hanging them on bushes to dry. It was there that my carefully hoarded personal supply of Kleenex and toilet paper ran out, a moment I had foreseen with dread. And it was there that I adjusted to, respectively, handkerchiefs and a container of water, the Indian equivalent of a bidet. The latter adjustment I recognized even then as a first-class achievement in Letting Go.

The desire to meditate came over me now and then, and I would sit down with a vague intention of concentrating or clearing my mind. Mostly I failed to achieve any calm or clarity and arose feeling disheartened. Once, standing before a human-sized stone figure of the seated Buddha near one of the stupas, I felt gently engaged by the stillness of the form. As I stood close and looked long, it seemed to breathe, and then we were breathing together, as one. Later, I told myself I had imagined it.

Part of me wanted to get back on the train and leave Sanchi, but another part ached for the unknown, the unknowable, without having any idea what that meant. I sat on the ground outside my room, watching the moon rise into a bank of clouds and wondering what I was doing there and why I wanted to stay.

In the book of Kabir poems, I read:

> *In your body is the garden of flowers.*
> *Take your seat on the thousand petals of the lotus, and*
> *there gaze on the Infinite Beauty.*

On my way back from a walk one evening, I stopped at a tobacconist's stall and bought a *biri*, a homegrown, handrolled cigarette. Since it came without the benefit of packaging, I did not really know what I would be smoking, which at the time contributed to its charm. At the Mahabodhi compound, the head monk was waiting for me just inside the gate. He invited me to evening prayer in the small temple. Sitting on the floor off to one side, I was self-conscious but pleased to be included. I wondered whether the swelling of my heart was in response to the exotic atmosphere created by altar, statues, incense, chanting, and the like or to the simple sincerity with which the monks performed their ritual.

Afterward, I went to my room and smoked the biri in the dark. I guessed that it was cut with ganja, or marijuana, which is sold along with tobacco cigarettes.

That night, I dreamed of a woman wearing a long yellow coat with a bold black zigzag pattern. She walked through the open iron gates into the Mahabodhi compound. A monk told her to go back outside, closed the gates, and said to her: "This time, look closely." The woman again walked toward the gates. As she reached them, the angular pattern on her coat matched up exactly with the black shapes of the bars. Then the blackness turned to nothingness; she passed right through, and what emerged on the other side of the gate was simply a pattern of yellow particles in empty space. In the dream, I had the dreadful sense that the woman was disintegrating. Then I recognized her as myself, and I was terrified. My only hope seemed to lie in finding the courage to be honest about what was happening. I searched my soul for the truth, then said distinctly: "I am afraid." The words appeared in the air as sharp black letters, repeating again the jagged pattern of the coat and the gate. Pattern, gate, words, I saw, were all the same: dramatic in appearance, but insubstantial.

After the dream, my days were perfused with strangeness, a mixture of apprehension and promise. I considered possible causes: traveling alone for too long, having no one with whom to speak in my own language about my experiences, or the weather, perhaps, which had turned dark and ominous. Then again, perhaps I was receiving some psychic energy emanating from that ancient center of spiritual power. Or maybe it was all from smoking the ganja biri.

One night, suddenly wide awake and unaccountably warm, with no thought or reason, I got up and bathed in the dark, under the cold tap. Then, thinking it might be near day-break, I sat and tried to meditate. The night wore on and on. I arose and found myself preparing to wash clothes. As I sorted things in the dark, my senses took me back to the hilltop; the sharp fragrance of lantana still clung to my garments. Uneasy thoughts about being in a sacred place filtered through my mind. What was I doing there? What *should* I be doing? Each time I tried to bring my attention back to the present, I noticed an alarming sensation in my chest, which made me wonder if I would ever be the same again.

Day arrived without dawn, which was obliterated by the heavy gray of the sky. I realized I had lost track of what day it was. I felt strange. I wondered if I was beginning to dissociate. Then I considered the opposite: maybe the strangeness was in being very connected—with my body, my physical needs; with the land, the past, the mythic; with spirit. But if that were so, it seemed to me I would find meditation natural and easy. Why was it so hard?

Kabir says:

> The moon shines in my body, but my blind eyes cannot see it.
> The moon is within me, and so is the sun.
> The unstruck drum of Eternity is sounded within me;
> but my deaf ears cannot hear it.

When I saw the head monk in the courtyard, I asked what they had chanted at the evening service. On a little notepad he printed in awkward capital ballpoint letters the Pali words for the refuge vows:

> Buddham saranam gacchami
> Dhammam saranam gacchami
> Sangham saranam gacchami.

Then he looked me in the eye, gave me the piece of paper, spoke the Pali words, and nodded to me to repeat them. He told me the words in English—something about taking refuge in the Buddha and his teachings—but the meaning slipped from my mind.

Early that morning, a busload of Nepali Buddhists had arrived at the guest house. I was glad for the distraction. The head monk relayed to me their invitation to accompany them to see the ancient sculpture in some nearby caves.

I was squeezed into one of the side seats behind the driver. Across from me sat a tiny Buddhist nun of indeterminate age, complete with shaved head and brown robes and a radiant grin. A boy in the back played a small drum, and everybody sang loud, happy songs. The bus bounced down country roads and then crawled through a village, dragging along a wriggling human fringe of vendors and beggars and children, while money and shouts and comestibles were exchanged through the open windows. As we left the village, people sitting near me insisted that I have some of the oranges and peanuts they had purchased. No one spoke English, but I felt comforted by the ongoing chatter, the music, the smiles and laughter, the sharing of food.

At the caves, the Nepalis gave the sculpture the most perfunctory inspection, saving their enthusiasm, it seemed, for the armloads of wild pea bushes they gathered along the way with great eagerness. These were carried back onto the bus, where the peas were shelled and eaten. Soon the aisles were deep in pea pods and leaves and branches, covering the layer of peanut shells and orange rinds that had accumulated on the trip out. Something about that struck me as wonderful. I experienced an unaccountable sense of freedom, an absence of self-consciousness, and a burst of love for Buddhism, which, I figured, was what made these people so nice.

Late that afternoon, I made one last visit to the hilltop. After a stretch of overcast days, the sun finally appeared, a gray disc low in the gray sky, exactly above the oldest of the stupas, like a living ornament. I lay on the stone wall and watched as it grew white and moonlike. Then dark strands of cloud blew across its face, and finally it burned through yellow, becoming sun. Once again, I followed the walkways around each of the stupas, those mounds of utter dense mystery that cannot be entered, penetrated, seen, or grasped, yet draw one in. Something swelled in my heart, and I felt a wrenching desire to stay there, against the knowledge that I would be leaving.

✧ ✧ ✧

On the train I talked with an Indian man named Sharad. I was showing him a pamphlet from the Mahabodhi Society when I came across the paper on which the head monk had written down the Pali words.

"He asked you to say these words, yes?" Sharad said. "And you repeated after him?"

"Yes. But I don't know what they mean—"

"Hah! You are now a Buddhist. You have taken vows of refuge in Buddha, dharma, and sangha. You did not know what you were saying?"

"Well, actually, yes. Now I remember that's what he said, but I didn't think I was taking vows. I certainly didn't intend—"

"Never mind. It is no special thing to become Buddhist or not to become Buddhist. But technically speaking, I think now you are Buddhist."

I tried to protest, but Sharad insisted that we all must submit to our karma, and clearly mine involved Buddhism. I dropped the subject, and then he said something even more perplexing.

"Now, if this bloody train makes it to the next station, you and I will be going away in different directions. "

"How do you know where—?"

"South, you are going, yes? Madras, yes?"

"But, how—?"

"You will be coming at some time to Bombay. I am giving you address of my cousin, who will know how to reach me."

I had not planned to go to Bombay, but as it turned out, toward the end of my time in India, it seemed like the logical place to spend my last few weeks. Somewhat reluctantly, I allowed Sharad to show me around, to take charge of my "program," as he called it. Soon I found myself submerged in a way of being that undermined any of my attempts to plan, to pursue goals, to live ahead of myself—the whole fixed forward momentum of Western mentality, which had been the unquestioned sine qua non of my life.

It wasn't that Sharad didn't plan. He made many plans, but they were continually revised and amended and superseded by new plans. Plans simply spewed forth from him as if he were wired up to a travel agency print-out system. We will go here, we will go there, we will meet a friend, we will borrow a relative's car, we must call the relative, we must locate the friend, we must purchase tickets. In the course of a day, none of the plans necessarily came to pass. Meanwhile, we enjoyed ourselves: we went here and there and saw other friends and rode in other cars and made more plans for the next day.

When, occasionally, one of Sharad's many plans was realized (by accident, it always seemed to me), things worked out remarkably well, with an undeniable ease and sense of rightness. Sharad and his friends and relatives and acquaintances seemed possessed of an uncanny sense about timing and making connections, being in the right place at the right time quite unexpectedly, against all the odds. I experienced it this way: after struggling with confusion, contradiction, loss of control—*Where? When? What? With whom?*—suddenly I would be released from chaos to find myself supported in an invisible net of vaguely related people and places that happened to come together, quite miraculously, at just the right moment. The answers to my frantic questions always turned out to be, *Here. Now. This. Us.*

When I told Sharad that I wanted to see the Ajanta caves, he arranged for me to stay nearby at the ladies' hostel at a college in Aurangabad. He said he would telephone a Mr. Shinday to alert him that I was coming.

Arriving in Aurangabad after a sleepless overnight bus trip, I found the rickshaw drivers at the station reluctant to take me to the college, which was outside the town. A combination of bullying and bribery finally got me a ride, but when the rickshaw stopped, I could see nothing that looked like my idea of a college.

"Mr. Shinday's house?" I asked the driver.

He pointed to one of a scattering of low concrete buildings, where a man in pajamas was sitting on the porch. Mr. Shinday did not come to meet me, but when I introduced myself, he invited me to sit down. Then there was an awkward period during which, reading between the lines of our polite exchanges, I realized that he had not received the call from Bombay. Mr. Shinday had never heard of me.

We sat together for a while, a very long while, I thought. Eventually, the head of the hostel, Miss Moray, was summoned. I was given into her charge, and we went to her room and sat again. I mentioned that I must make arrangements if I was going to see Ajanta in the little time I had. Miss Moray replied that everything would be taken care of, that arrangements would be made.

After some time, Mr. Shinday appeared, dressed in shirt and slacks, and suggested that I might like to see the rare books in the college library. I was relieved to get into familiar territory. The librarian, Mr. Gamre, was overjoyed. He seemed to have been waiting lifetimes to show his collection to someone who cared. His manner suggested that my presence was almost too good to be true: as a foreigner and a teacher of religious art,

I might bring to his lonely treasures the appreciation they deserved. The library assistant was sent scurrying for large portfolios, which Mr. Gamre opened reverently before me.

I had settled into enjoying myself when Mr. Shinday intervened, saying that it was time to move on. Mr. Gamre implored him to let me stay. They argued, discussing my program, and its regrettable parsimoniousness, as if I were not present. Mr. Shinday prevailed, and an unhappy period followed in which I sat in his office while various people were consulted in the development and revision of my itinerary. I felt like a prisoner.

When I finally returned to the hostel, I was exhausted, frazzled, and desperate for solitude, a bath, and bed—only to find that the electricity and water were off. Not that it mattered, because the entire female student body, about fifteen girls, were waiting for their chance at me. A lantern was brought into my room, I was escorted to the single chair, and the girls squeezed together in clumps on the bed and the desk. Questions, both polite and embarrassingly personal, were put to me. My very ordinary belongings were extravagantly admired. Songs were sung and poems recited and a dance performed in my honor. I tried to pretend that it was all as wonderful in the moment as I knew it would be in retrospect.

I had asked the nightwatchman to wake me early so I could get into town in time to catch the bus to Ajanta. When I was awakened, though, it was by a rooster's call. I leapt out of bed and into my clothes and dashed furiously past the sleeping nightwatchman on my way out. Although I had been assured that arrangements had been made, no rickshaw was waiting outside. I walked to the main road, anxious about missing the bus and angry about being smothered with solicitousness when I did not need help, then neglected when I did.

I stood in the road, not knowing what else to do. After a while, a boy on a bicycle appeared. When he motioned for me to get onto the handlebars, I took it to mean that he had been sent, not to worry by whom. With one hand I clutched a small bag in my lap, and with the other I clung to the handlebars. We wobbled and fell after a few steps. The boy produced some string and lashed my bag to the back fender, then indicated that I should remount. I grimly resumed my awkward perch, trying not to succumb to the waves of hatefulness and humiliation that rose in me. Slowly and uncomfortably, we rode to town.

Finally, we came to buildings and wider streets and even traffic, of the sundry sort common in India. As soon as I caught sight of the bus, I got down, yanked my bag from the fender, thrust a wad of rupees into the boy's waiting hand, and ran, propelled by a near-ecstasy of relief.

A familiar figure stood with the bus driver: Mr. Gamre. He greeted me primly, saying that he had come to lend me his own special book on Ajanta. But it was clear that he was there also to look out for me; he had coaxed the bus driver to wait until I arrived. At that moment, Mr. Gamre might have been the manifestation of some local deity who helped foreign tourists and other lost souls find their way to Ajanta. I sank gratefully into the front seat that had been saved for me, caught once again in the great net of Indian interconnections.

At the caves, the guide spoke with obvious feeling about the spiritual nature of the place: its conduciveness to contemplation, the devotion of those who carved the series of temples from the living rock, the divinity shining through the faint remains of wall paintings. Inside one of the large caves, to demonstrate the resonance of its spaces, he chanted, so sweetly that people were visibly moved. I asked what the chant said. He repeated the refuge vows:

> *Buddham saranam gacchami*
> *Dhammam saranam gacchami*
> *Sangham saranam gacchami.*

I take refuge in the Buddha
I take refuge in the Teachings
I take refuge in the Community of Followers.

That night, back at the ladies' hostel, I made no mention of needing a rickshaw early the next morning to catch my return bus, and no one mentioned it to me. I awoke in the night, sensing that it was time to leave. The electricity was off again, and I could not get the lantern lit. Feeling my way in the dark, I went to the communal bathing place, a row of spigots set over a trough. The water was running, and I had a private, if chilly, bath.

I lightened my load by leaving some books and clothes and toiletries for the girls, hoping this was one of those parts of the world where it is appropriate to present an admired object to the admirer. Then I felt my way out of the building, step by careful step, to the road.

It was astonishingly dark. I could make out the shapes of trees and roofs against the sky, but the ground below was pure blackness. I considered the unpleasant things my feet might encounter. Cow dung. Or cows, which sleep in the street. People sleeping in the street. Snakes. Rats. Other nocturnal creatures. Other kinds of dung.

I hoped I could trust living things to sense my approach and move aside or at least to make a noise to alert me to their presence. As for dung, if the damage to my shoes was sufficient, well, I could just leave them behind. My step became less tentative. And if, barefooted, I stepped in something? Why, it was simple—I would wash my feet. But where? I laughed aloud. The first place I found some water, of course! In the meantime, I would just walk on.

Soon I was proceeding at a jaunty pace through the blackness. It felt different from anything I had ever experienced— like walking on air, that free. Whenever I arrived would be all right. If I was early for the train, I would wait. If I was late, I would catch the next one. I realized, with a thrill, that there was nothing to fear.

$$\diamond \quad \diamond \quad \diamond$$

Looking back, it seems as if Sanchi marked some undefined threshold on my spiritual path. During the rest of my travels in India, opportunities to let go came my way at every turn. At times, I clung desperately to my self-righteousness about how things should be, clung to my resentments toward a country known to inflict manifold trials and tribulations on those who travel there. But, little by little—by force of circumstance, I would say—some of my certainties were pried loose, or at least softened. As a result, I began to put less effort into trying to make things happen, and I became more interested in seeing what *would* happen.

Repeatedly, I got the feeling that many Indians had intuitive capacities beyond anything I had believed possible, for example, that they really did know a certain amount about where I was going even when I did not know myself. That may or may not be true, but something I glimpsed then—a different kind of knowing—took hold of me. To pursue that was far more compelling than seeing yet another new place, and it meant that I began to shift my focus to the inner world of awareness.

ASIAN OUTPOSTS

IN SILENCE: WALKING MEDITATION

With eyes lowered and aimed directly in front of me, as instructed, I watch the carpet remnants pass underfoot. Red tweed. Gold and brown pile. Avocado shag.

I lift my gaze slightly to the bare brown feet of the Burmese man ahead of me in the line of people practicing walking meditation. At the beginning of this retreat, the Burmese man said he had never meditated before. But from the easy way he puts each foot down—step, step, step—I suspect this comes far more naturally to him than to me. I watch the softly swaying hem of his striped sarong.

Without my being aware of it, my eyes drift upward. I see a framed certificate relating to the recent establishment of this temple. Several posters with Buddhist emblems. A photograph labeled "The Palace Site, Mandalay."

At some point, realizing that I have passed the photograph four times and read the caption four times, I lower my eyes again.

Step. Step. Step. Sensation of foot on carpet. Subtle differences in softness, thickness, texture. Step. Weight shifting forward, back foot lifting. Step.

Objects in my peripheral vision tug irresistibly at my awareness. I decide to relax the rules a bit and allow myself to look at whatever I pass that is reasonably close to my feet and below waist height. On the floor next to the altar is a small lamp with a shade made of green string. A brass gong in a wooden frame. Along the side wall, an electric fan and a six-foot-long piece of orange pegboard shaped like a dog biscuit.

Step. Step. Step.

The bare lower stretch of the back wall startles me into looking up. Near the ceiling is a square electric clock with a red plastic strip across the bottom proclaiming in punched block letters, THIS CLOCK WAS DONATED BY SAM.

Five minutes after 4:00. Or rather, five minutes and fifty-eight seconds . . . tick . . . tick . . . ah, six minutes after 4:00.

Thank you, Sam. Your thoughtful gift is much appreciated. I can tell you that is the one item in this room that everybody wants to look at. I find it indispensable. How else would I be able to figure out that a single lap at this pace takes about sixty-six seconds, so in half an hour we will make just over twenty-seven circumambulations, or fifty-five in an hour? With that information, I can count time by laps instead of by clock watching, or, when that gets boring, check laps against the clock to gauge our speed.

4:11.

I abandon the effort to concentrate on walking and give myself over to mental agitation. Forty-nine more minutes. I don't know if I can stand it.

With each pass by one corner, I glance toward a record cabinet on which is displayed a Nike shoe box emblazoned with another red plastic strip, this one bearing the message, MAY BLESSINGS GO WITH YOU. Please, I think, please—next time around, please let some blessing drift down and clothe me in peace.

My desire to look around becomes intense. The only way I can bear to stay in this room, I tell myself, is to feed that craving. I look. My eyes are ravenous, devouring.

When I have satisfied my curiosity about the other people and the wall decorations and have had enough of carpet remnants and clock games, it is only seventeen minutes after 4:00. There is nothing left but to look at the altar.

Furtive, sidelong glances reveal three tiers jammed with Buddha figures, candles, incense, plastic roses, an NFL tumbler half-filled with water, a green ceramic elephant, two black urns supported by what appear to be inverted Jell-O molds, a philodendron trailing from a wine carafe tied about the neck with a fat piece of blue yarn, a metallic tree with heart-shaped aluminum-foil leaves that send shimmers of light across the room every time a car passes outside. At either end of the altar stand long-handled fans, maroon with gold decoration and block lettering that says, THE BUDDHIST TEMPLE, NASHVILLE, TENN., U.S.A.

This altar is not beautiful, by any criteria I know. It's an esthetic catastrophe, in fact. But I love it. I am sort of in love with it, with its very weirdness. There is something so touchingly sincere about it, and within that, I have to admit, I see an odd kind of beauty.

CHAPTER 1

MONKS, MEDITATION

**IN A CULTURAL SETTING THAT IS SOFT AND SWEET,
MEDITATION ITSELF PROVES ARDUOUS.**

I returned from India to a new life in a Midwestern city, where I did part-time editorial work in a small publishing company while I considered career options and the general purpose and meaning of life. My job required me to be on time, and I bought a new watch to replace the one that had stopped in Sanchi. That act symbolized my reentry into the world of drivenness that I had managed to let go of while I was in India. The hard life, I called it, as in the opposite of soft.

A notice about a five-day meditation retreat appeared in my mailbox. The retreat was to be led by a Burmese teacher, the Venerable U Pandita, and would be held at the Buddhist Temple in Nashville, Tennessee. Enclosed with the notice were a newsletter, handwritten in three South Asian scripts with a typed English translation, and a blotchy photocopy of a newspaper article. "North Edgefield Baptist Church Becomes Buddhist Temple," I read.

The church building had been long empty and dilapidated, the article said, when it was purchased by a Burmese American named Min, who arranged for and oversaw its conversion. The temple had been in operation for several years, complete with monks dispatched from Burma (now Myanmar). It served as a cultural and religious center for the Southeast Asians in the Nashville area, mostly Laotian and Cambodian refugees. Buddhist holidays, the newsletter stated, were celebrated there with a good crowd, and, in traditional Asian style, dedicated laypeople brought food each morning for the monks.

I soon learned that, like most American church- and synagogue-goers, the Asians attended primarily to participate in services, to celebrate holidays, to "make merit" (the Buddhist equivalent of earning stars in one's heavenly crown), and, of course, to socialize. As is generally true anywhere, most members do not seek radical personal transformation.

The Westerners who were drawn to the Buddhist Temple, however, came to learn meditation, and their interests and those of the Asians overlapped little, if at all. For the one group, going to the temple is largely a cultural experience. For the other, it is profoundly personal—the seeking of enlightenment. I did not think of myself as aiming quite that high, but I knew, without actually making a decision about it, that I would attend the retreat.

❖　❖　❖

Across the river from Nashville's most conspicuous architectural monument, a replica of the Parthenon—across the river, that is, from most of what is grand and glittering, in an area that is hardly even presentable—yes, indeed, a Baptist church had been born again as a Buddhist temple.

A world away from the Greek-style edifice, the temple stood obscurely at a corner two blocks off the interstate highway, in a borderline slum of shady streets with decaying wooden houses and cinderblock projects. The temple shared the general desolation of the neighborhood, its lower ranges lost in the long-unchecked growth of thistles and Spanish needles and weedy trees-of-paradise, the lot encircled by a rusty chain-link fence topped with barbed wire.

But in my memory, and in the photograph I still look at now and then, something inscrutably majestic lives on in those architectural bones. The facade rises grandly from a high, stepped platform, and paired columns flank deeply recessed doorways. In the round-arched windows, opalescent stained glass glints like mosaics of jade and turquoise and aquamarine. Above the main entrance, almost hidden by a tree, an inscription in fine, deeply chiseled Roman letters reads, NORTH EDGE-FIELD BAPTIST CHURCH. At the opposite corner, a smaller entrance is boldly labeled in fat black painted letters, BUDDHIST TEMPLE. While the building's architectural features suggested to me the noble truths of Western civilization, its immediate appeal lay in something new and exotic taking hold within those walls—what I thought of then as the Asian view of the world, with its sweet, silent insistence that there is more to life than we know.

✧ ✧ ✧

The front was the building's good side. From the rubbled area that sloped toward the back, I could see broken panes in the sanctuary windows. The roof had caved in on a side wing, leaving not an opening to the heavens (which might transform an edifice into a grand ruin, by association with the Parthenon), but only a dead cascade of old building materials, gray and brown and messy. The rear of the main building, originally housing the church hall, offices, and Sunday school rooms, was intact but neglected. The only clue that it was in use was a small sign handlettered in bright orange. Posted in the middle of a wall and pointing nowhere, the sign said

MONKS
MEDITATION.

The only door in sight was locked, but there was a bell. Inside was Asia.

For someone already in an advanced state of equanimity, the initial encounter with the temple might have been easy. For me, the pervasive strangeness induced mild culture shock. As soon as I entered, the outside world was thoroughly closed off. A narrow hall ran the length of the building, jogging here and there, through a warren of mostly empty rooms. It felt subterranean. The few rooms that were occupied had the dingy, too-lived-in feeling of places inhabited by men without women.

The first room was designated by a construction paper and magic marker sign as the "Office," in quotation marks, the word traced with two colors in the curlicue cursive of people who grew up writing a South Asian script. The space was furnished with a Formica table, chairs, a couch made of several mattresses stacked and covered with an Indian bedspread, and a card table holding a percolator, heavy china cups and saucers, and enough boxes of tea and artificial cream and sweetener to last several lifetimes. The kitchen, across the hall, was crowded with staples from an Asian grocery, stacked on and under the counters. A note on the refrigerator read: *"Please remind to close the bottom door because it is not normal. Thank a lot."*

Down the hall was the room used for meditation. Signs beside the door, in an Asian script and in English, requested "Please Remove Shoes" and "Nobel Silence" (the illustrious name, in its association with the world's great achievers, sounding more noble, these days, than plain old "noble").

As each of us arrived for the retreat, we were directed by a monk to put our belongings in one of the empty rooms. The three women were assigned to a large room across from the meditation hall, where we staked out our spots and spread out our sleeping bags. From a stack in a corner, behind a large artificial Christmas tree, we each took a folding chair to serve as a combination towel rack and bedside table.

I envisioned the room in its former incarnation filled with Baptist cherubs chirping Bible verses, its walls decked with pastel pictures of handsome Jesuses—Among the Children, In The Garden, Confounding The Elders. I knew from my own childhood how it must have looked: shelves with paste pots and dime-store scissors, an attendance chart with colored foil stick-on stars, stacks of flimsy Sunday school magazines called something like *We Are His Sheep: A Weekly Study Guide for Young People,* an upright piano from which a sweet lady fervently led such favorites as "Thaaat's the B-I-B-L-E!" Now the room was empty even of its ghosts—not the Buddhist void of All, but the dreary, tired emptiness of disuse.

Several of the men were given small, narrow rooms that originally must have been church offices. With a single recessed window and a cot, each room looked as if it had been just waiting to reincarnate as a monk's cell. The other men chose rooms along the hall closer to the meditation room, but being sensitive, perhaps, to the power of monastic example, not too near the women.

A few of the ten people who came to the retreat brought to it pretty much what I had, namely, keen interest and not much experience. Francie, a lanky college student, had never meditated at all. Others, however, were seasoned meditators. Carole had been practicing her own form of meditation for years. Dark and handsome and a little mysterious, she had about her a look of fully realized spirituality. What does she expect to get from this, I wondered, if she is already there? And Francie—to all appearances healthy, bright, attractive, too young to have run up against any of the pitfalls of life— why would she want to spend five days doing something she had not tried for even five minutes?

Three of the men in the group had studied meditation in Asian monasteries. Clay had gone to Thailand for that purpose and was one of the first Americans to obtain a long-term visa for Burma. Steven had been there in the Peace Corps and had stayed on to study meditation. Paul, retired from the foreign service, had been posted in Southeast Asia for many years. Keith was a psychologist who taught a course on consciousness and wanted to know more. Jim and David were longtime meditators; they had driven across several states, as I had, to attend this retreat.

Min, although he had had no experience with meditation, was also participating. An enterprising sort, he was involved in numerous projects in addition to his teaching job. The most notable were the Buddhist Temple and a Thai restaurant, which his wife was managing.

To those of us who had been in the East, the temple seemed like a bit of that exotic world transplanted halfway around the earth. South Asia: with its overabundance of people and animals and deities and even time, its richness of color and fragrance and taste, its appalling insufficiencies, its persistent hint of other dimensions of existence, that world had maddened and enchanted and changed each of us, so that, one way or another, we could never forget it. And here we were, once again, in this unlikely setting.

✧   ✧   ✧

Noon, when the retreat was scheduled to begin, came and went.

In the office, Paul and Keith sat down with bowls of the monks' midday meal of rice and vegetables and talked about Bangkok. Clay sat cross-legged on the mattress couch and spoke in Burmese with one of the monks.

While we waited, I asked Steven what he knew about this kind of meditation. U Pandita, he replied, was a renowned spiritual leader, properly addressed as Sayadaw, meaning "great teacher." The Theravadan, or Southeast Asian, tradition of meditation is called "vipassana," which means "insight." The teaching of vipassana meditation came to this country mainly through several Americans who had studied in India and Thailand and Burma in the 1960s and 1970s, then returned to establish a meditation center in New England. U Pandita's presence in this country offered a rare opportunity for vipassana students to work with one of the greatest living masters of the tradition.

Min was in and out. Warm and personable and relaxed, quick to laugh and joke, he strode about in a cowboy hat and sun-sensor glasses, making introductions, making arrangements, making things happen. He announced, with a grimace and then a grin, that we would follow monastic routine: rising at 3:30 A.M., with walking meditation at 4:00, sitting meditation at 5:00, breakfast at 6:00, then, after an hour for personal hygiene, continued sitting and walking meditation, with an hour for lunch, a talk by the teacher in the evening, and more meditation until bedtime at 10:00 P.M. Following monastic tradition, no evening meal would be taken, although the hypoglycemic and otherwise desperate could have some fruit juice. Silence was to be kept. Reading and writing, which involve mental "noise," were prohibited.

I considered the strangeness of what we had embarked on. I thought I felt a thrill of collective anxiety sweep through the room.

At 1:00, Min bustled in to say that things were running a little late, then bustled out again. At 1:30, he reappeared to say that the retreat would start at 2:00. Each of the men who had lived in South Asia left briefly and returned wearing a cotton sarong that is ordinary dress for men in that part of the world. Then word passed that U Pandita had arrived. His attendant quietly appeared in the office, a lithe, handsome man wearing a sarong and a T-shirt with the legend "Bangkok Rolls Royce Motor Works."

Two o'clock came and went. Finally, Min himself appeared in a sarong and herded us all into the meditation room.

It was a comfortable size for the ten retreatants, plus a few monks. On the floor, wall-to-wall carpet remnants lapped over one another in visual cacophony, with a strip of lavender crushed velvet laid across the front as if to soften this onslaught where it approached the altar. The altar was arranged in the style of the resplendent temple altars one sees in travel posters of Thailand, with tiers of religious effigies and liturgical paraphernalia. Here, however, the more-is-more esthetic was achieved by an effulgent display of largely mundane objects, prominent among them plastic roses stuck into half-gallon diet cola containers, all entwined with multicolored bubbling Christmas tree lights.

From an assortment of cushions stacked against a wall, we each took one and chose a spot on the floor. Then we sat and waited. Five monks filed in: a line of shaved brown heads, looking from the back like giant nutmegs, mounted on voluminous russet robes draped over one shoulder and leaving the other bare. The monks bowed several times toward the altar and arranged themselves in the front of the room, then sat quietly, looking blank. Nothing happening. Nobel silence.

After several minutes, Min cleared his throat and introduced the monks. They were U Jotipala, the abbot of the temple; two other resident Burmese monks who looked very young; a former resident, a Nepali, recently transferred to a monastery in California; and a Sri Lankan, who was older and larger than the others, with prominent features and a prepossessing air. The monks made no response as Min pronounced their names, just continued sitting, relaxed, benign. Then the Sri Lankan turned and beamed at the door as U Pandita Sayadaw strode in.

The Sayadaw also sported a shaved head and russet robe but was distinguished by heavy black-framed glasses, a burly physique, and the stern mien of a drill sergeant. He made his bows and settled onto the two cushions set for him at the center. Then he looked out at us and frowned.

The retreat, U Pandita said gruffly, with the attendant translating in soft, fluent English, would start with our accepting eight precepts to be followed for the next five days. Two of the prohibitions, against causing harm and against taking anything not given, are variations of the Judeo-Christian Commandments not to kill and steal. The others are monastic vows: chastity, sobriety, silence, not eating after midday, the renunciation of personal adornment and of "high, luxurious beds." Keeping that last precept was not going to be a problem at the Buddhist Temple, but nobody laughed.

U Pandita went on to describe the basic technique of vipassana meditation. One sits with eyes closed and places attention on the breath, and when the attention wanders, notes the activity of the mind. Sitting meditation alternates with walking meditation, which is done very slowly, with the attention placed on the movements of the foot in taking each step—lifting, moving, lowering, placing—and the gaze directed at the floor just ahead. The meditator aims to note what is happening at each moment: physical sensations, emotions, thoughts, whatever is experienced. The process sounds simple, but, as I already knew, it is wildly complicated by our habitual mental activity. I thought with trepidation about my previous sporadic efforts.

The purpose of the practice, U Pandita was saying, is to become cognizant of our mental habits and to develop mindfulness, which is the ability to maintain direct awareness of experience. He closed his eyes, took a deep breath, and exhaled slowly. His face softened. He opened his eyes and looked at each of us. Mindfulness, he said, is like breathing in fresh air: healthful, joyful, suggestive of the full, deep experiencing of each moment that is the heart of this path. Even though our concentration may be weak at first and time is short, each moment, he assured us, presents an opportunity for mindfulness. If proper effort is maintained, great progress is possible.

He described the procedures for meals and personal interviews. Then he wished us a good retreat, bowed, and exited, followed by the monks.

Silence, except for soft suspirations and an occasional cough and the sounds of cars passing outside—and the interminable chatter of the mind, the maddening, lifelong conversation with oneself.

We sat from 3:00 until 4:00. Sixty long minutes. Toward the end, my muscles, bones, and nerves strained together in an intense yearning to move, to stand up or lie down or stretch or merely shift position. Oh, when will this be over? I must not be doing it right. This is agony. Everybody else . . . I can't . . . if only . . . how much longer?

When, at last, the much-anticipated moment arrived, we gingerly straightened our legs, stretched, stood, and moved into a circle around the perimeter of the room. I looked surreptitiously at the others to see how the walking was done. Keith hobbled, his knees still stiff from the sitting. Francie walked like a ballet dancer. Carole seemed to have her eyes closed; with her hands clasped at her chest and her chin lifted, she wore the rapt expression of a medieval saint. This is easy for her, I thought, it comes naturally, whereas for me. . . . Even among the sarong-wearers, some lifted-moved-lowered-placed their feet mechanically, while others walked more naturally. I aimed for something in the middle.

Quickly, though, I forgot all about walking and instead took advantage of the chance to look around as we circled the room. If the point of all this effort was to develop visual awareness, I would be a superstar, I thought, as my eyes devoured the makeshift efflorescence of the altar. But meditation? I had almost immediately abandoned the effort to pay attention.

When the walking period was over, I was glutted with observation, guilty at having neglected to note the sensations of walking, and so, so relieved to return to the cushion. Ah, to sit, to still the mind . . . but, even in sitting, my mind raced on. Soon I was eager to walk again, vowing this time to keep my eyes on the floor. I imagined how intent and yet peaceful I would be, how focused my awareness, how graceful my step, how light my spirit. . . .

But I was off again, drifting far from the present moment.

Mostly I was irritated with myself, but sometimes my irritation fixed on U Pandita. He had said that our schedule was the same as that followed at his temple in Rangoon, while implying, I thought, that concessions were usually made for Westerners. Our wimpiness in these matters—sitting on the floor, keeping still, concentrating the mind, enduring austerities—must be well known. I spent long minutes hating being considered a wimp, and hating being one. I tried to decide which was worse, failing to notice that, in either case, the hating felt the same.

On the other hand, I developed an inordinate fondness for the largely unseen beings who sustained us in our dreamlike existence within the temple. In occasional forays outside the meditation room (to go to the bathroom or to meals or to interviews with U Pandita), we glimpsed monks gliding through the hall, answering the telephone or the door, nodding and smiling, as dignified and graceful as cats. Assorted Asian laypeople, mostly women, also appeared now and then, bringing provisions for breakfast and lunch, tidying up, laughing and chattering with one another and with the monks, offering us polite greetings, even though we only smiled back in response. I felt immersed in the strangeness of foreign speech, writing, dress, race; surrounded by some softness, indefiniteness about things Westerners treat as hard and precise, the inevitable something inscrutable.

Our challenge was to stay intently focused on the details of immediate, concrete experience: physical sensation (the sponginess of the carpet underfoot, knee and back pains from sitting in one position for a long time, the taste of food); emotions (anger that one's concentration is not better, self-pity for having to endure greater suffering than anyone else, happiness at getting into bed, fear of talking with U Pandita); and thoughts, always thoughts (Why am I doing this? How much longer until we walk? When I get back to work . . . Maybe I should try TM.).

I noticed all those experiences, but my predominant mental activity was daydreaming. Typically, I began with the situation at hand and developed it in imaginary directions, thus effecting my escape from my present misery. My favorite self-entertainment featured the Buddhist Temple as a missionary operation. The monks ran this foreign outpost primarily to tend their expatriate flock, the Southeast Asian refugees. The retreat, though, was in response to specific needs of Americans, people whose successful manipulations of the material world have provided them with no spiritual sustenance. U Pandita comes here just as Christian missionaries have gone to other continents, to bring light into darkness, to bring the Buddhist version of the Good News: there is an end to suffering.

(But *when?* Eleven more minutes to sit. Then an hour of walking and another hour of sitting before lunch. After lunch, six hours until the talk, nine until bedtime.)

Back in my daydream, I figured that for the monk-missionaries, this place must be a hardship post. Our culture presents difficulty and deprivation for them. Compared with the slow time of an old, traditional, tropical, religious society, our frenzied life might tax the equanimity even of a Buddhist monk. They are prepared, though, to endure much in offering their teaching where it is most needed. They look upon our plight with compassion. Even the Burmese ladies who bring food to the temple—

I envisioned them as part of a gentle effort directed toward our salvation.

And we? We are benighted primitives with no tradition of investigating and accepting responsibility for our own mental states.

But then the daydream would dissolve, because at that point, the analogy breaks down. Instead of conversion to a set of beliefs, the path of meditation requires practice, endless practice. Sitting, walking, trying again and again to simply look, taking nothing on faith, always examining one's own experience, asking, *What is happening here, now?*

CHAPTER 2

LOTUSES IN THE RIVER JORDAN

WE COME TO OUR SEEKING AS CHILDREN:
INNOCENT, PURE-HEARTED, UNTRAINED.

The daily interviews with the Sayadaw had something of the awesomeness of Dorothy's encounters with the Wizard of Oz. You entered the presence of a powerful, enigmatic personage whose being seemed to partake of another dimension, and who therefore might lift the veil that obscures the meaning of your own. You approached with fear and humility and hope. Sometimes U Pandita was like a great bald head, and all you could see were the thin, dark slits of his lips and eyes across an immobile face. Sometimes he was a blaze of fire, brilliant, blinding, searing away at your confusion and weakness. Sometimes there was only emptiness: brown robe, brown skin, a form—but nobody home.

When it was time for your interview, you were summoned by one of the monks. During a walking period, the monk would appear in the hall and catch your eye as you turned a corner to face the door. Then he would glance downward with a slight sideways twitch of his head to signal that you should leave the file and follow him.

These breaks in routine glowed with allure. Simply leaving the room, walking at a normal pace down the hall and up some stairs into a different part of the building was anticipated as high adventure after hour upon hour upon hour in that same space. And talking—to describe one's suffering and effort, the personal melodramas relived repeatedly in one's mind, and to seek guidance from a renowned spiritual teacher—that was an enticing prospect indeed.

Sitting on the floor outside U Pandita's inner sanctum while I waited to be called in to my first interview, I indulged in the urge to lean back against the wall in a comforting slump. Ahhh. Quiet. Time passing.

Getting uncomfortable. I sat up straight for a while. Time still passing. At one point, I realized indignantly that so much time had passed that I might as well have been meditating. But then I relaxed again into the fact of nothing happening, still just sitting, sitting, sitting, with the same old inescapable mental chatter.

The door opened, and Francie came out. I tried to read in her face some clue about what had transpired, but she seemed turned inward, and I saw nothing. The attendant, with a soft gesture like silence in motion, indicated that I should enter and be seated.

The Sayadaw sat cross-legged on a cushion atop a platform. The attendant sat on the floor at the side and directed the interview. I sat in front facing the platform, and at the attendant's prompting, stated how many hours I had spent in sitting and how many in walking, then described what had happened in that time. U Pandita asked terse questions to determine my progress, corrected mistaken ideas leading to improper practice, and, in what sounded like perfunctory mumbles, urged me to pursue the path with the utmost patience and persistence.

I do not remember anything more about what either of us said, only that Sayadaw showed no interest in my melodramas, offered no sympathy for all my suffering. Then it was over. The attendant indicated that I should bow and ushered me out. Though I felt as if something had happened in those few minutes, I had no idea what.

✧ ✧ ✧

Each twenty-four-hour period was punctuated by distinct high points: sleep, food, evening talk, and interview, pretty much in that order of attractiveness, at least for me. Sleep and food, being in shorter supply than usual, I anticipated as pinnacles of pleasure. Some people, it is said, can sleep in meditation posture, but I am not one of them, and several times I sneaked out during walking periods for a nap. Francie also took to her sleeping bag at one point. Carole, though, seemed calm and energized and centered. She spent precious time each night penning notes in a journal. Her higher degree of holiness, I figured, exempted her from the prohibition against writing.

Remarkably, considering our sleep deficits, nobody stayed in bed past the 3:30 A.M. bell. Perhaps the mere thought of food fueled our resolve to meditate for the two and a half hours until breakfast. Breakfast was happiness itself. We could share the rice soup brought in for the monks (sweet or spicy, on alternate days) or help ourselves to dry cereal and fruit. Then we could begin thinking about lunch, a feast of Thai dishes, delivered from the restaurant by Min's wife. At noon we walked slowly to the kitchen and selected one of the carry-out Styrofoam cartons marked "spicy," "no spicy," and "middle spicy" and "veg" and "non veg." We took them into the meeting room and sat in silence around a big square table. Thinking of the eighteen hours until the next breakfast, we ate enormous quantities.

Anticipating the evening talk got me through the long afternoon. U Pandita in translation could hardly match the Baptists, those masters of the inspirational, but our accumulated deprivations made us an eager audience. By the end of each day, having spent the better part of the preceding twenty-four hours enmeshed in inner turmoil, we welcomed reminders of what we were doing and why. Each talk lasted twenty minutes, the length of time (we learned later) that U

Pandita had been told Americans were able to pay attention. After the talk, he answered questions. Except for Clay and Min, who sat with their legs to one side, Burmese style, and Jim, who was a Zen student and maintained impeccable upright posture, we sprawled about the floor, leaning on our elbows, acutely, effortlessly attentive. Francie, with the easy unselfconsciousness of youth, lay on her back.

U Pandita's teaching style was based on the ancient tradition of enumerations and similes and parables. The Four Noble Truths. The Five Hindrances. The Twenty-Seven Factors of Enlightenment. How the mind is like a monkey, how it is like a cow in a field. He proffered anecdotes based on ordinary life in an Asian village and made mystifying pronouncements about ridding oneself of defilements. I did not know exactly what it all meant, but it did make me feel that my agonies were not without purpose.

By the third day, everyone seemed to have relaxed a little into the grueling routine, the oppressiveness of time, the insignificance of our agitations, and the endlessness of our inner commentaries. We also figured out what clothes were most comfortable. Francie and I changed from jeans to loose cotton skirts, and Min appeared in pajamas—most comfortable of all, and, from an Asian point of view, socially acceptable in this informal situation. He sat in front of me, so I had the opportunity to study his pajamas at length. They were handsome, gray with dark red piping. Why don't we wear pajamas all the time? I wondered.

Min disappeared for a while during the afternoon, then returned during the last period before the evening talk and sat down in the front facing us. Looking uncomfortable, he cleared his throat and quietly announced that we would break the silence for a brief discussion. No one said anything or moved, except to turn their eyes toward him.

"Ah . . . you must understand," he said carefully, "U Pandita have not been in this country before, and it is . . . well, it is very different from what he accustom to in Burma."

Silence. It becomes habitual more quickly than you would think.

"Many thing we take for granted here, in Burma people don't do." Min adjusted his pajamas. "These thing don't matter to me because now I am American just like you. But U Pandita, not only he is from Burma, but he live in monastery, his whole life almost, and in monastery there is certain way everything is done. In Asia, there is more respect for teacher than here. I am teacher," he laughed, "so I know. In Asia, we are very careful to show respect to teacher, and since you don't know this way of ours, I think now somebody must tell you, because I think you want to show respect to U Pandita."

We regarded him intently.

"One thing we do is sit in respectful posture for dharma talk. 'Dharma' means Buddhist teachings. We want to show respect for dharma, so dharma talk is not time to relax. Especially it is very disrespectful to lie down, and most disrespectful of all is to put feet out toward teacher."

Exposing the soles of the feet to someone's face, Min explained, is as rude in Burmese culture as spitting is in ours. We had committed other infringements and faux pas, which he mentioned gently. Francie still wore her earrings, thereby ignoring the prohibition against personal adornment. A more grievous impertinence had been unwittingly committed by Keith. On the second day, after much wriggling and shifting and sighing, he attempted to solve the problem of physical discomfort by stacking five cushions on top of one another against a wall, with one behind his back, to make a reasonably endurable seat. But U Pandita's two cushions—the second a sign of respect, to elevate him above the rest of us (shades of

The King and I!)—had been mocked and belittled by this grand throne that sprang forth from Yankee ingenuity.

Francie removed her earrings, and Keith moved to a single cushion.

Carole raised her hand, and Min nodded to her. Hesitantly, she said that in the interviews, U Pandita seemed distant and disapproving.

"The first time, I described what I experience in the meditation I've developed on my own, which is . . . well, I just let my mind go and sort of enter this incredible space of peacefulness and bliss." She sighed. "But he didn't like that. He said, 'No bliss.' That's what he said. 'No bliss.' He said the way I was doing it is 'wrong practice.' And so he instructed me in the vipassana technique, and now I'm trying that. Today I really wanted to explain to him how it's going, but he seemed totally unresponsive. I actually felt he was determined to avoid looking at me, you know?"

I had had the same impression. Francie and I joined in, and a soft plaint rose, an age-old cry from the feminine heart. *He doesn't even look at me,* we said.

"Ah," said Min, grinning. "A monk is not suppose to touch women, or even look at them. You can imagine how he feel when he come here and women are so free, and . . . well, you know what I mean. It is very different, very different."

Carole lifted her black hair from her neck and pulled it over one shoulder. "Well," she said, "I kept trying to make eye contact, and I guess I was getting pretty intense, because finally he did the oddest thing. He picked up this piece of paper—it was the notice about this retreat—and he held it in front of his face. And I know he wasn't reading it because I could see through it, and it was upside down!"

Min laughed and pushed his glasses up on his forehead. "I think I know what happen. Sometimes Buddhist teacher hold special fan in front of face when they give teaching—one of

these fan, like there beside the altar. Mostly now for decoration, but sometime teacher use fan to mean it's not teacher who
is important, but teaching. You understand? When you go to
talk with U Pandita, you do not talk to the person, you go to
listen to the teaching. In Buddhist religion, a highly realized
teacher, like U Pandita, he is not there, in a personal sense. No
one is there. Just the teaching, coming through that body."

Relief, and the beginning of some tiny understanding,
spread through the group.

"He is not hiding from you, but showing that you must not
try to talk with him as an individual. This is the Buddhist
way. Don't take it personally. I cannot tell anything about
Buddhist philosophy, I don't know any more than you, but I
think this is important. Anyway, I want to tell our customs of
respect, and now you understand, I think."

Little nods all around.

"So I think everything okay. Too bad we have to interrupt,
but better if we all talk and understand. Right? Any problem?"

Keith said that it was all well and good that meditation
was like letting fresh air into the mind, but what about letting
some fresh air in the meditation hall?

Min said he would look into it. "I also am trying to meditate, but at the same time I must be in charge and do things like
a janitor. I have never meditated before, either. Only time I
was ever in monastery, I was seven years old. This is what all
boys do in Burma, they are ordained as monks for a week. I
learned nothing then. This is just as hard for me as for you. So
I forget I am wearing two hats, janitor and meditator."

That amused us. Faces opened into smiles.

"So we go back to silence. I am sorry I must make some
noise now. I try to open windows before dharma talk."

He returned with a screwdriver and a hammer and a
stepladder, which he set up next to the altar. After days of
watching nothing but our own minds and the immediate sur-

roundings, we gazed with hungry attention. Seeing Min mount the ladder in his pajamas and fiddle with the windows was as fascinating as a circus. With a few bangs and grunts, he pried one of the windows open about an inch. The others were painted shut. We watched wistfully as he climbed down, folded up the ladder, and left with it tucked under his arm.

✧ ✧ ✧

At the dharma talk that evening, we sat respectfully, in our upright postures. We were midway through the retreat, and with the End no more distant now than the Beginning had been a few days before, survival suddenly seemed assured. This put a new perspective on things: enlightenment rather than endurance became the issue. Time seemed short, even precious, if we were to gain something from it all, attain some shred of illumination.

As U Pandita settled onto his cushions facing us, a hand went up, and he glared and nodded slightly in that direction. Clay requested that the dharma talk be extended beyond twenty minutes, explaining that we would gladly sit and listen for as long as U Pandita spoke and that we were eager to hear his teaching.

The attendant started to translate, but U Pandita's Buddha face had already broken into a smile.

"Oh-kay," he said.

A laugh burst from the group on hearing him respond in English. He chuckled, too. Then he spoke for more than an hour. It was partly in Burmese, partly in English, and clear in a way that had little to do with language. I remember best his succinct demonstrations of pure awareness.

Make fists, he said, showing us what he wanted. *What do you know from that experience?*

Silence, then a few wrong answers. "Power," one man said. U Pandita gave a dismissive jerk of his head. "The strength of my hand," ventured another. No response.

Then Carole spoke. "Hardness and tightness."

U Pandita's eyes flashed. He nodded. *The experience itself.*

All we know, directly, from making a fist is how it feels. Everything else is added-on association. In that pure experience—the very hardness and tightness, knowledge that cannot be transmitted to another person—one discovers the true nature of things, the source of wisdom. With wisdom, one enters a profound, harmonious calm in which one is no longer thrown off balance by the vicissitudes of life. Attaining this state, U Pandita asserted, is the most important thing we can strive for.

Whether because of our improved comportment or the determination we had demonstrated by sticking it out or our desire to glean something from the remainder of the retreat, the communication between teacher and students flowed with ease. The lecture became a discussion, and in our exchanges, a rapport developed, almost an intimacy. U Pandita frequently silenced the attendant. He seemed to understand what was said in English and often responded with enough English of his own to get his meaning across. He even made jokes. After the strain of silence and seriousness, laughing together was a tremendous release. I was touched by the sense of reconciliation, and at moments I was close to tears. We had crossed the halfway point in the retreat, and we had also crossed a chasm of cultural misunderstanding.

For the last two days, the attendant announced, we could do walking meditation individually, wherever we wanted to. At the end of the hallway, I discovered a door to the outside. In the bright sunshine, the weedy side yard looked like the Garden of Eden. I sat on a warm stone step and felt physical comfort for the first time since the retreat had begun. Carole came out and sat beside me. We talked softly. She had shifted to the vipassana technique with little trouble and had established an easier relationship with U Pandita.

My meditation continued to be fraught with difficulty. I had occasional moments of peace, which kept me going, but mostly it was agony. Each time I reported to U Pandita, he said I was not doing it right, and I returned to sitting with increasing desperation. Mentally I gritted my teeth and determined to follow my breath, whatever it took. But no matter how dogged my effort, my attention drifted.

As I lay in bed one night, my mind raced uncontrollably, images and thoughts assailing me in a terrifying torrent of energy. I thought I would never go to sleep. I thought I might be going crazy. The next day, I told U Pandita about it in my interview. That happens as a result of trying too hard, he said. Do not worry. If you cannot sleep, place your attention on the sensations of your body touching the bed. Let it rest there, and you will relax. And remember to be gentle in your sitting.

❖   ❖   ❖

On the last day, we arose to find the premises occupied by a small army of Burmese families. They had arrived during the night in carloads from as far away as Chicago and Cincinnati. The main purpose of U Pandita's visit, it turned out, was not to instruct us but to ordain seven Burmese boys.

The temple was transformed. Those still, silent rooms and hallways were filling with people and activity, talk and laughter, and, already, the pungent aromas of cooking. Here was another Asia. The newcomers wore Western clothes, looked well-to-do, and addressed us in excellent English. Somewhat unnecessarily, word was passed that the silence was ended.

Soon everybody began moving through the hall toward the meeting room where the boys waited to have their heads shaved. Two of the monks donned glasses and took up straight razors, and mothers and sisters held cloths below to catch the hair. Everyone else stood around in a circle. In the center, the monks worked deftly, and clumps of black hair fell silently from the new nutmeg heads. A home movie camera rolled.

Then everyone traipsed back through the hall to the meditation room. We retreatants were shy: now we were the foreigners. We stood tentatively around the doorway, looking in. The space where, for those long days, we had sat on our cushions in neat rows, walked in an orderly clockwise file, and struggled with our souls in that timeless silence now vibrated with movement and sound. The cushions were pushed here and there as family groups established their encampments. Teenagers lolled around the base of a pillar, and mothers with babies congregated near the door. The boys to be ordained sat at the front, their eyes lowered modestly.

The monks entered, bowed, and took their places at one side. U Pandita addressed the group in Burmese and read from some dog-eared pages in a rapid monotone. It got boring very quickly, the exoticism evaporating into the tedium inflicted on such occasions, it would seem, by all religions.

Finally, the reading was over, and the monks rose with a soft rustle. The boys got to their feet more awkwardly and held out before them the folded robes that signified their entry into the fraternity. The monks took the cloths and draped their new brothers, winding the long cotton pieces in an age-old pattern.

Then U Pandita spoke, and Min explained in English that there would be a final talk upstairs in the sanctuary. Everybody got up and filed through the hall and up the dusty stairs to the main floor. Stepping into the sanctuary I felt for a moment as if I had gone to heaven. Light, color, space, in such limitless abundance—it felt the way Easter morning is supposed to feel.

In fact, the place was something of a shambles. There were ominous cracks in the plaster of the walls and ceiling. Jagged holes of daylight ruptured the glorious expanses of the windows, and jagged pieces of opalescent glass littered the floor below. The oak pews, though, stood stable and solid, unscarred by the ravages of time or the crime that marked the neighborhood. We filed in and sat. American style.

A huge altar, a grander version of the altar downstairs, displayed a host of Buddha statues, from a larger-than-life gilt effigy in the center to little plastic equivalents of the Jesuses and Marys that dangle from rearview mirrors, with a full complement of vases, urns, bottles, glasses—the whole gaudy array. Half hidden behind the altar was the baptistery. On the wall above the baptismal tank was painted a pastoral scene showing the River Jordan, with shepherds and sheep and lavender hills and blue sky with puffy clouds, in the familiar style of long-forgotten Sunday school books. Into this landscape the new tenants had inserted their own imagery: lotuses, exotic wading birds, and a skillfully rendered elephant, drinking from the river—all aimed, one would guess, to make the place look a little more like Burma.

Oh, North Edgefield Baptist Church: what of all those good Christian souls who sat here in your heart, and, exhorted from the pulpit to mend their ways, rejoiced and repented and sang songs and gave money? What would they make of your reincarnation, and of this assembly? Brown-skinned families hearing words they have heard countless times and our motley group, striving to grasp the meaning of those words with the earnestness of children encountering something utterly new. . . .

U Pandita presented the fundamental teachings. The attendant translated into formal English. Min, his enthusiasm high in the doubly happy occasion of the retreat ending and the temple fulfilling its purpose with such an illustrious teacher and a congregation drawn from far and wide, his volubility welling up and over its usual level, interjected his own translations in colloquial American.

Dukkha, says U Pandita.

Suffering, says the translator.

"This mean dissatisfaction," says Min. "The unsatisfactoriness of our life. 'I can't get no satisfaction'—right?"

The Americans laughed, so the Burmese laughed, and even our solemn Sayadaw seemed to experience a momentary spasm of mirth.

Dhamma, says U Pandita.

Truth, says the translator.

"Dhamma is Pali term, dharma is Sanskrit," Min explains. "Meaning Path or Way or Law, like Law of Nature. All those same as Truth, and in Buddhism our goal is to see truth. Dharma also mean the teaching of this Path."

U Pandita smiled and nodded. The work of the mission is proceeding, I imagined him saying to himself.

I conjured up his Western counterpart, a bishop, perhaps, visiting a small foreign mission that serves a group of Americans in a remote part of China or Korea or Burma. A young American pastor operates the mission, which offers social as well as religious functions for the expatriates. A growing number of the native people are also interested in the religion. Their customs are such that they do not fit in well at ceremonial occasions; they spit in public and squat on their heels and bow to the pastor. Their desire to learn, however, seems genuine. In fact, they are drawn to the most radical parts of the gospel, like the Sermon on the Mount. They are excited about seeing the bishop. Word of his visit spreads by some invisible means, and many villagers show up to receive his instruction in the faith. They are as innocent and eager as children. The bishop recovers from his initial shock at their manners and is impressed by the freshness of their desire. Such is the power of the spirit, he reflects, that it takes root even in this unlikely corner.

Oh, unlikely corner, two blocks from the interstate in Nashville, Tennessee, where behind a rusty chain-link fence and a thicket of weed trees, a grand space opens up, and people walk among shards of stained glass as if their path were strewn with jewels and sit and listen to holy teachings by one who has magically come to resemble a kindly, loving priest, the shepherd caring for his flock, and the space swells and glows in the soft natural light that seems to transmute all garishness and decrepitude and illumine the manifold ordinary and extraordinary beauties: who is to say that the Parthenon in all its glory—originally painted in garish colors, housing an overlarge gilt effigy—was arrayed in greater spiritual splendor?

✧ ✧ ✧

Well, such is the fruit of sensory deprivation. Postretreat euphoria is a common phenomenon.

U Pandita led a two-month retreat in New England and then returned to Burma. He seemed to leave a vacuum (if a Buddhist monk can be said to do such a thing) that quickly filled with stories about how formidable he was, how fierce his approach to meditation. Go-for-broke enlightenment, people called it. He does not care if you die sitting on the cushion, they said; he would see that as a noble demonstration of your devotion to the path. People talked about surviving the New England retreat as if they had earned the Buddhist equivalent of a Purple Heart.

Perhaps that was part of the attraction: U Pandita offered a rare opportunity for heroism. He became the hot ticket among the U. S. vipassana meditators, and a good number of the foremost American teachers beat a path to Rangoon to sit at his feet. In *Inquiring Mind*, a newspaper that goes out to the vipassana community, a cartoon referred to this minimigration in the form of the old classic sequence of roadside signs:

WHEN MIND GROWS WILD

    LIKE HAIR ON FACE

        SAYADAW SAYS

           COME TO MY PLACE—

              BURMA SHAVE.

CHAPTER 3

SAMSARA AND NIRVANA

PURE PRESENCE PROVES MORE POWERFUL THAN WORDS.

Implausible as it may sound, the truth is that I had fallen in love with the Buddhist Temple. My thoughts about it, mostly fantasies, had that familiar obsessive quality.

In relation to the temple, I imagined myself in two roles. In the first, I brought to it a special appreciation, seeing the true grandeur of the building, the levels of meaning in its architectural detail. The exquisite moldings around the entrance, for example, or the delicate frieze below the main pediment—an elaborated version of the famous triglyphs and metopes of the Parthenon—represented the highest achievements of Western culture. That such a building was occupied by Asians, by monks (missionary monks, of course, in my mind) was not merely incongruous but deeply significant.

I also felt concerned about the vast difference between what I took to be the temple's aim and its limited means. I could see myself helping to make the place a little more presentable, bringing in other people to restore the building, teach English to the monks, raise money, whatever needed to be done. This picture was based in the energetic, can-do, forward-thrusting approach of which the West is acknowledged master.

The second role in which I saw myself was practically the opposite. I would be the student, the humble recipient of what Asia had to teach. I would be saved.

✧ ✧ ✧

After the Nashville retreat, I began to talk on the telephone with Jim, whom I had met there and who lived an hour away from me. Jim often traveled elsewhere in the country to study with Buddhist teachers, and he had been practicing meditation regularly for years. He became a great source of information for me in what was, at that time and place—the Midwest in the early 1980s—something of a spiritual void.

Jim had first meditated with a Zen group, but he felt that the brand of Buddhism was not important. We agreed that the most appealing thing about Buddhism is what it isn't: you don't have to belong, you don't have to believe, you don't set other people and faiths outside.

"What's important," Jim told me, "is that it's a practice. It's something you *do*." He advised me to find a regular group to meditate with.

For almost a year, I sat at the local Zen Center. Each Sunday, at 5:45 A.M., I rushed to my car with a cup of hot tea that spilled onto the dashboard as I broke the speed limit to get to the 6:00 meditation. I learned the formal routines: removing shoes on entering, bowing, sitting on the cushion and turning around to face the wall, doing the slow walking meditation, receiving tea, chanting. Sitting on the cushion, I followed my breath, daydreamed, berated myself for my lack of concentration, and waited for something wonderful to happen as a reward for showing up on time and sticking at it week after week.

As for the dharma talks, I understood little of what the teacher said, less because of his Japanese accent than because of the inherent difficulty of comprehending Zen. The topics of the talks were very abstruse, it seemed to me, the teacher's favorite being "dependent origination." I struggled to understand, but as the months went by, my need to know dwindled.

Winter was especially hard. Wearing a pea coat, muffler, hat, and gloves, I felt like an overdressed bag lady, while the advanced students sat calmly in handsome Japanese robes. When I asked about heating the room, one of them pointedly described a monastery in Japan where it is so cold in winter that the monks' exhalations leave condensation trails.

In other seasons, I suffered the chill of emotional isolation. I was the only woman, and the only one who asked questions.

"What does 'form is emptiness, emptiness is none other than form' mean?" I asked after we chanted the Heart Sutra.

Feeble laughter from some of the sitters, a benign smile from the teacher, and a well-worn statement about needing to experience it directly, not through words.

"What does *gate gate paragate parasamgate* mean?" I ventured on another occasion. Those words, at the climax of the Heart Sutra, are marked in the chant by the ringing of a special bell.

"Cannot be transrate into Engrish," the teacher said politely, shaking his head.

Other than *dharma*, the only Sanskrit words I could remember were *nirvana*, meaning total enlightenment, and *samsara*, meaning regular life, with the implication of suffering. The teacher assured us that nirvana and samsara are the same—a typically mind-bending Zen paradox.

When I offered to help the teacher with a translation project, I was informed that someone else had that job. When I offered to learn how to set up the elegant little altar and to bring flowers for it—which was what I really wanted to do—the response was the same. I told myself it was good for my ego to keep silent, to keep sitting, to tough it out.

The positive things that happened at the Zen Center seemed so trivial that I discounted them. Each week, for example, after the two hours of sitting and walking meditation, when tea was served, I experienced a quick elevation of mood. I suspect others felt it, too, and for the same reasons. First, moving out of the formal sitting posture gave an automatic boost to the spirits, and second, the tea, a strong Japanese brew, provided a welcome stimulant hit. One could interpret this as a "high" resulting from the two hours of meditation, but I credited the caffeine. This high was supplemented by a sugar kick from the cake made by the teacher's wife. She used a different cake mix every week, and against the sameness of our routine, the variety was very agreeable. My favorite postmeditation diversion was watching the man who served tea stride solemnly in his heavy black pleated skirt, under which, through a gaping side slit (he was thick through the middle) I could see the bright patterned print of his boxer shorts—like the cakes, a little something different to look forward to every Sunday.

I also found it amusing that the Americans strove so sternly to emulate the faultless comportment demonstrated by our teacher, performing every movement with excruciating economy and precision and earnestness, while the one student to behave naturally and unselfconsciously was the only other Japanese. Large and dark, with long messy hair, he drew attention to himself in what seemed to me a most un-Japanese manner. His bows were perfunctory, and, sitting on the cushion before the first bell rang for meditation, he would stretch and yawn. While we waited for tea to be served, he would lift his cup and examine it intently, turning it this way and that, rubbing his thumb over the bottom, almost caressing it. He drank noisily and, after polishing off a few pieces of cake, emitted a series of appreciative belches.

That final half hour of tea and cake and human foibles cheered me so much that by the time I left each week, I could convince myself that it was all somehow worthwhile. But the following week would bring another hour and a half of misery.

When I did learn something at the Zen Center, it was usually incidental, outside the formal teaching situation, almost as if I had to be caught off guard for anything to get through my defenses. The most memorable example involved a little blond boy who appeared one week. When I arrived, the boy was poking around in the outer room near one of the regular sitters, a blond man. I assumed they were father and son. After the bell was rung for the first sitting and the room had settled into stillness, the boy came inching along the wall we were facing. I braced myself for the father's reprimand, but nothing happened. The boy ran his fingernails across the wall for a while, making a scratching sound, then walked between the rows of sitters to the other end of the room, clop-clop-clopping his shoes. Finally, with a prolonged creaking of hinges, he opened the door to an adjoining room and played there, audibly, through both sittings. I spent the whole time feeling irritated and resentful, with intermittent bursts of pity for the child and the parent, who, I imagined, shared some difficult, desperate life together.

After the sitting, the teacher began his talk by saying, "Today we had little boy in room, moving about, making a noise."

Suddenly it did not seem so terrible. At the end of the talk, the blond man left alone, and the boy went off with someone else.

I felt a shock at seeing my assumption, my certainty, my little drama evaporate into nothing. I also felt a scary thrill of "not knowing." In realizing how much I did not know, I saw how not knowing is inevitable, how it is simply in the nature of things. I was aware, too, of how all my thoughts and feelings about the boy only caused me distress, how unfounded and unnecessary they were, how potentially destructive. But at the time, I did not know what to do with that insight. I did not yet see how meditation offers a clear space from which to examine and question such reactions, to see how entrenched they are in our mental habits, and how they draw us away from the simple sufficiency of each moment.

Maybe I was looking for an excuse to quit, because when I read a news article about organizational style in Japanese businesses, something clicked shut in my mind. In any Japanese group, the article said, all members know their places and accept authority, and nobody asks questions. Aha! I thought: my problem with this Zen Center is simply that it is too Japanese. The next week, I went to meditation as usual, but when I left that day, I knew I would not return. Whether it was because the place was too Japanese or too masculine or too cold or just too impenetrable, I no longer cared. If ego made me quit, I told myself, so be it.

❖ ❖ ❖

The names and addresses from the Buddhist Temple retreat in Nashville must have gotten entered into some American Buddhist database, because I began receiving notices for other retreats. The first to be held where I lived was a weekend with a vipassana teacher from Thailand, Achan Sobin. Jim was going. He had attended several retreats with Achan (meaning "teacher"). I was filled with happy anticipation. On home ground, with more realistic expectations and even some experience, I might have a better chance to make real progress in meditation.

On the day the retreat began, I arrived early to set up cushions borrowed from the Zen Center. At the top of a tall flight of stairs, a small brown man dressed in white was standing and smiling.

"Oh," I said, "you must be Achan." I climbed the stairs with my armload of cushions and introduced myself. Not knowing whether to bow or shake hands, I tried both and lost control of the cushions, one of which rolled back down the stairs. Achan laughed, putting me at ease, and tried to say my name. He seemed to have difficulty understanding the sounds and visualizing the word.

"Sara, as in 'samsara,'" I said.

Achan laughed delightedly at my joke. He practiced my name a few times, and we bowed and shook hands and bowed again. He insisted on retrieving the cushion at the bottom of the stairs, then helped me set up the room. What a sweet man, I thought, relieved not to feel intimidated by a spiritual teacher.

The public was invited that evening to the opening dharma talk, entitled "The Way of Mindfulness." During the first few moments after Achan began to speak, a silent shock filled the audience: his difficulty with English was such that to grasp even part of what he said required the utmost concentration. He struggled especially with adjacent consonants, pronouncing each one separately. "Mindfulness" was a real mouthful. For "mind" he said "my-nn-duh," making it three syllables, and we strained to compress the sounds back into a word. But something about him was so compelling that the room vibrated with palpable yearning, a collective effort to understand so powerful it might have moved mountains. By the end of the talk, most of us could not have related much of what Achan had said, and yet we knew something we had not known before. The Way of Mindfulness seemed to have drifted invisibly into the room and settled there among us, filling the air we breathed, inspiring us with calm attentiveness.

When those who had come for the talk had left and there were only those of us who would sit the two days of retreat, Achan gave us meditation instructions. They were much the same as those given by U Pandita, about following the breath and noting the contents of the mind. Achan also recommended labeling whatever experience draws the attention away from the breath. If you hear a car go by, you say to yourself, "hearing, hearing," until the attention returns to the breath or is drawn elsewhere. Walking meditation was different in that here we walked separately, each person staking out a pathway around or across the room. But it was the same lifting-moving-lowering-placing of the feet, and the point was the same: to be aware of every sensation, every movement, everything that happened in the body and the mind.

As the lights were turned down for the first sitting, Achan smiled beautifully; he appeared inordinately happy. I took one last look at him and suddenly saw that his white outfit was not some official holy garb but a machine-embroidered Thai shirt and American sweatpants. That was somehow reassuring.

I closed my eyes. The room felt comfortably dim and quiet and cozy. I could sit here forever, I thought. Before the sitting period was over, however, I had convinced myself that hours had passed instead of minutes, that Achan had lost track of time, and that I was a fool not to say something. If an experienced meditator like me was in agony, no doubt someone new must be . . . did my awareness make me at least indirectly responsible? . . . if only somebody else . . .

The bell sounded softly, cutting off the raging mental chatter and filling the universe with that sweet, clear, oh-so-welcome sound: *tinnnnng.* . . .

In the precious few seconds between sitting and walking, I surveyed the other meditators. They rose from their cushions with various degrees of inelegance, like insects whose metabolism has been slowed by the cold. Then we walked, in solemn slow motion, one drawn-out step at a time, lifting-moving-lowering-placing. At the sound of the bell, we slowly returned to our places and settled onto our cushions to sit some more.

Achan's special emphasis was on maintaining attentiveness not only in sitting and walking meditation but in all movement—rising from the cushion, resuming the sitting position, eating, going to the bathroom, going to bed, waking up, every moment throughout the day. He also taught standing meditation. "Ssuh-tahn-deen," he repeated patiently, as we all stood there. ("Sutton Dean," I heard, and thought of an investment firm.) Eventually, his pronunciation matched up in our minds with the meaning he intended. Standing. Standing. Standing.

Most of the retreatants followed the vipassana style, which makes numerous concessions to comfort, including shawls or blankets in which one swaths oneself (quilts, comforters, duvets, even sleeping bags and light rugs are also used) and small pillows that can be stuffed around to support knees or ankles or hips, all of which hide a multitude of postural lapses. Jim alone sat Zen style, on the edge of a regulation black cushion, back straight, hands forming a circle at his center, elbows out (as if you are holding a raw egg in each armpit, they say), chin in, eyes open but lowered, and unmoving.

Achan met with each of us for personal interviews and gave dharma talks twice a day. In the first talk, he explained *nama* and *rupa*, name and form—the knowing of "hearing," for example, and the experience of it.

"What is sitting?" he asked, then answered, "*Rupa*, or body, is sitting. Who knows sitting? *Nama*, or mind, knows sitting." He urged us to attend to the distinction.

I had no idea what he meant. When he went on to talk about experiencing impermanence, no-self, and the inevitability of suffering, I felt close to despair. In my interview, I told him I did not know what I was doing, I felt completely lost, and I burst into tears. He laughed softly, and I cried harder, undone by his gentleness, by his not reacting in the way I had expected.

"This is not right attitude," he admonished sweetly. "This is only samsara. You know samsara, yes? Your own name! Suffering of life. Only illusion. In meditation we see through illusion." We talked about striving—striving is not Right Effort, he said—and I began to see that, once again, I was trying too hard.

As I left, I realized that I had been unaware of Achan's accent while we talked. Indeed, I had had the sense that between us there were no barriers to communicating the deepest, subtlest movements of the heart and mind. I was aware that I did not know Achan as a person, not the way I knew other people, but I had no question that what I felt was love.

In the dharma talk on Saturday night, Achan outlined the sixteen steps to enlightenment, twelve mundane and four supramundane, according to Theravadan tradition. He assured us that in the course of the retreat we would take some of those steps. I did not believe it; I could not accept myself as a serious candidate for enlightenment. My fear was that I was trapped in some submundane realm and that Achan knew that but was too nice to mention it.

For the last sitting on Sunday afternoon, Achan asked us to forget everything we knew about meditation technique. Forget following the breath, forget labeling thoughts, and simply sit. I felt a rush of relief. I just sat, still and content, with no concern about what I was doing or why. Just sitting felt fine.

When Achan struck the bell at the end of the period, I did not even change position. I still just sat, while he gave a short closing talk. But when he began to ask us questions about our progress, my anxiety returned.

Did anyone have the experience of impermanence? Several people raised their hands.

Did anyone have the experience of no-self? A Catholic nun raised her hand.

Did anyone have the experience of suffering? Everyone laughed, including Achan.

"Everyone understand *nama* and *rupa?*"

No one said anything.

He explained a little, assuring us that we knew the experience, and hands went up.

"So, *nama* and *rupa* everyone learn," he said with satisfaction. He looked at me. "Yes?"

"No," I said weakly.

"No?" He smiled. "I think you know *nama* and *rupa*. So simple!" I shook my head.

We went back and forth for a while until it looked as if I might cry again, so Achan settled for saying that I knew it but did not realize that I knew it.

When the retreat was over, Jim and Achan helped me pick up the cushions. Jim said he was staying in town another day to take Achan sightseeing, and they invited me to come along. I was pleased; it might be a chance to rectify the poor impression I had made. Also, since the main thing I had gotten from the retreat, I figured, was the sheer inspiration of Achan's presence, another day with him might offer some real spiritual advancement, and without having to endure meditation.

Overnight, however, I became apprehensive about being around a spiritual teacher off the cushion, so to speak. I was fearful that getting to know Achan more personally might alter my view of him. Even scarier was that he might get to know me outside my role as a meditation student. Who, then, would I be?

I lay awake much of that night worrying about what to wear the next day and how to act. I wanted to appear attractive but not frivolous, sincere but not solemn, natural but in no way unseemly. I wanted Achan to recognize my affection for him, but not to mistake it for . . . well, the other, grasping kind of love. I wanted to know him as a person, but I did not want to jeopardize my view of him as a teacher. An endless parade of dualities passed through my mind—this is desirable, this undesirable—presenting me with an endless series of troubling possibilities if I did not get everything just right.

The next morning, Achan was dressed in a bright blue leisure suit (clearly he had not stayed up worrying about my opinion of his clothes). As soon as he was installed between us on the seat of Jim's truck, Achan asked about the retreat in Nashville and our opinion of U Pandita.

That was far from the kind of topic I had expected us to talk about. Jim, however, launched into an account of our retreat, including how the women complained that U Pandita ignored them.

Achan giggled gleefully. "He is monk! All his life he not with women, cannot even look at them. So here is very different for him."

"Was it difficult for you to deal with women when you first left the monastery?" Jim asked him.

"So difficult!" Achan chortled. "American women so . . . free. You know? Take time for me to understand. Long time."

I felt then that Achan's attitude was not proper for a spiritual teacher. I took his laughter to be schoolboyish, as if the subject of women were slightly naughty, and I even imagined that he enjoyed the notion that his Burmese colleague might have been discomfited by his first encounter with oh-so-free Western women.

Now I see it quite differently: the ideas about "naughty" and "discomfited" came from *my* mind. I had no evidence that Achan's attitude was anything but completely open and lighthearted. My confusion, my unexamined judgment, came partly from the fact that I had so rarely experienced complete openness and lightheartedness. In fact, I would say that I had witnessed those qualities consistently only in Buddhist monks. Achan (who was no longer a monk when I met him) was something beyond my ken. As a man, Achan was too good to be true, and so my mind readily generated a little story to make him something I could manage: a naughty schoolboy.

The great thing about being around open and lighthearted people is that those very qualities act as subtle encouragement to drop the negative habits of our minds and to be open and lighthearted ourselves. That was fortunate for me on that occasion, because the day did not work out as I expected, and in other company, I easily could have felt resentful. Not only did we not discuss meditation, but what Achan wanted to see was all the most obvious monuments on the tourist track. He mingled gaily with Midwestern farm families and conventioneers and teenagers, and although his accent, or my awareness of it, had returned in full force, it did not seem to inhibit those conversations. He spoke at length with a group of evangelical ministers, making no mention of his own religion, and somehow they all seemed to be talking about the same things. Being around him made me feel that everything was really pretty simple; something in his very being made goodness and gentleness and generosity seem only natural.

At the Botanical Garden, Achan was less engaged by the natural world than I had expected. I wondered if he was getting bored and feared that he might want to go to a theme park, which seemed more his style. The only thing at the garden that stirred his interest was a mirrored building that reflected trees, bushes, lawn, and, in the distance, the three of us. That was the kind of house he would like for teaching, Achan said emphatically. When he taught, he would sit inside. He could see his students, but they could not see him, only their own reflections.

Jim nodded and smiled, and then they both laughed.

By mid-afternoon, I was finding sightseeing nearly as grueling as a meditation retreat. We were running late, but when Achan saw an ice cream store, he wanted to stop, and so we did. Jim drove slowly as the three of us licked our cones and tried to say our good-byes at the same time. I felt a surge of feeling. Love? Longing? Or attachment?

What is the difference between those things? I put the question to Achan as he stepped out of the truck. He laughed and laughed, as if I had told a good joke. "Woolly woolly sotto," he said several times. He was still laughing and waving when we drove off. "Woolly woolly sotto!"

"What did he say?" I asked Jim.

"He said that your question was 'Very, very subtle.'"

That night I dreamed of working at something I loved, of carrying out a series of simple tasks and feeling profoundly fulfilled. It was not that the work had any great purpose or special value but merely that I found pleasure in it; it suited me so perfectly that I felt no separation between me and what I was doing. I woke before dawn, smiling, having known in my dream the experience of constant joy.

✧ ✧ ✧

In a long telephone talk with Jim, I asked a lot of questions. What had Achan meant about students looking at him and seeing only their own reflections? What was it about Achan that made me feel different in his presence? And why did everything about him still seem so ordinary? What *is* the difference between love and longing and attachment?

"I think," Jim said, "the only way to find such answers is in your own meditation."

I felt a pang of frustration. "But I've tried all these meditation techniques, and no matter what I do, it seems to be wrong. Mostly I just daydream. Maybe I'm getting something out of it, but nothing that makes me very happy. I don't really like any of the things I see about myself. In fact—"

"Hey, look, self-knowledge isn't exactly good news, you know."

"Oh? I guess I thought—"

"You thought you were going to discover that down deep you're a pure and holy person?"

"Well, sort of, yes. Isn't that—?"

"You know, a lot of it is finding out what meditation isn't. Like feeling peaceful all the time—no way. Also, it's not just concentration. Most of us think of meditation and concentration as the same thing, and we try to get concentrated and our mind wanders and we think we've failed. But somewhere down the line we get it that that's not it. Then we may have other mistaken ideas and eventually realize it's not those either."

I waited for him to finish, but he said nothing.

"Well, what *is* it?" I finally asked. "Aren't you going to tell me what it *is*?"

"I don't know," he began. "But I think . . . I think it's very simple. I think it's just about coming back to the present moment."

What kind of answer is that? I wanted to say.

"Or here's an idea I like," he went on. "You know how some electronic systems—computers, furnaces, things like that—are designed so that the system shuts down if something goes wrong, then you press a reset button to start it up again? That's a great metaphor for understanding meditation. It's as if our awareness, our being present, is always shutting down. We drift off, we leave the here and now, but we can come back any time, in an instant. All we do is reset and come right back to the present. It takes hardly any effort at all—less effort than being elsewhere."

I sighed. "Sometimes I think I'd do better just trying to make a go of samsara. Then I talk with you, and trying for nirvana actually seems like a reasonable pursuit. But I wonder if the only way I'll ever get anywhere with meditation is to give it a hundred percent."

"I just heard about something you may be interested in," Jim said. "A meditation retreat center in western North Carolina. It's called Southern Dharma. A brochure just came in the mail. I've got it right here. They've got some good teachers coming. I'm looking at this schedule . . . hey, the first one's a woman. An American woman Zen teacher."

After we talked, I checked my mail and found that I had also received a copy of the Southern Dharma brochure. The mailing address was a rural delivery route outside a town not far from my grandparents' cottage where I had spent summers growing up. My parents had retired nearby. North Carolina felt like home. I thought about what Jim said: an American teacher. A woman.

Then I walked slowly through the house, returning my attention again and again to the sensations of movement, resetting to the present. Jim was right—it was easy. But then I would feel the tug of habit toward getting things done, and the countermovement toward preferring to do something else, and the downward spiral of feeling guilty and torn, wondering why I did anything, what it all meant, the fear that I was somehow doing it wrong.

I think it's just about coming back to the present moment, he had said. *And you can reset to the present at any time.*

In the kitchen, I picked up an apple and a paring knife, went out to the back porch, and sat down on the bottom step. I cut the apple in half, then into quarters, and trimmed the core from each quarter. A seed fell onto my foot. I flicked it onto the ground and stubbed it into the dirt with my toe. Then I ate the apple and sat looking out into the trees. Again and again, I returned my attention to what was before me. No need to do anything, no need to think at all.

Suddenly, I was struck with the awareness that what was there, right there around me, the fullness of the present moment, is all there is. And it is everything: all existence is present, myself part of it, and it is all *right there*. A long laugh tumbled out of me. It seemed terribly funny that we should try so hard when everything is already here.

For days I could return to that perception at will, when I remembered to pay attention, and the world seemed fresh and rich and startling in its completeness. Then, gradually, the vividness faded.

My interest in pursuing spiritual practice, however, stayed with me. Spending time at a place dedicated to contemplation just might, I hoped, rouse in me the requisite commitment to sitting still and silent on a cushion, observing my breaths coming and going. I read the brochure from Southern Dharma, every word, over and over.

❖　❖　❖

A few days later, my mail included an invitation to the Zen Center picnic. I wondered why I had been invited, since I no longer went there for meditation. Maybe it was a mistake, and my name had simply not been removed from the mailing list. But maybe it was a subtle way for the teacher to let me know that he bore me no ill will. If he could push the reset button, as it were, I figured that I could too.

Walking into the park, I saw the group from a distance, settled onto blankets spread near the edge of a pond. Perhaps they sat more easily on the ground than your average Midwesterners, but they looked like any all-American picnic, a mix of people in T-shirts, shorts, sunglasses, and baseball caps, amid a scattering of coolers and paper cups and plastic containers and children. The regular sitters were there, more human in the company of family and friends. It turned out that the Japanese student, the one who wriggled and belched, taught ceramics and was also a performer with a traditional Japanese taiko drum group. The teacher chattered happily in Japanese with him, beaming now and then at everybody and urging us to eat more potato salad and miso noodles and barbecued taco chips and something with seaweed.

After lunch, drowsiness settled over us. The adults sprawled on the ground. The teacher sat soft and still, looking cool in the summer heat. The older children went off a little way and played softball, their shouts and squeals a distant, happy song.

The drummer sat on a log. A two-year-old girl crouched on the ground not far from him, drawing in the dirt with a stick. She drew a big, shaky circle, then moved a few inches and drew another. With her tiny pink and white dress upended over her diaper, she crept, like a crab wearing a bonnet, toward the log. When her stick swung near the drummer's foot, she stood up and looked at him. He smiled. She smiled and sat down beside him.

He picked up a stick of his own and motioned to her to go on drawing. They worked away side by side, two figures, one tiny and pink, one big and dark, both leaning forward at the same angle to draw in the dirt. Two ponytails sticking up, one a bunch of curly blond wisps clamped with a pink plastic butterfly, one thick and black and straight, tied in a bandanna. Tiny ruffled pinafore next to muscled bare brown back.

The drummer turned a paper cup upside down on the ground and drew his stick around it to make a perfect circle, then showed the little girl. She grinned. He drew another and another and another. She bounced and giggled. When paper-cup rings covered the ground in front of them, he sat up straight for a moment, then sprang into the air with a shout, landing in a low crouch in the middle of the circles. His head level with hers, he looked her hard in the eye and gave her a daring smile. She laughed, then with a yell jumped next to him. They danced, each in turn following the lead of the other. They scuffed their feet in the dirt, shrieking with wild pleasure, getting onto their hands and knees to obliterate the remaining traces of what they had so perfectly drawn.

When they tumbled spent on the ground, the teacher pointed at them, grinning. That, he said, looking around at all of us, is the true meaning of Zen.

CHAPTER 4

KISSING A WEEPING WILLOW

THE ROAD TO SPIRITUAL PRACTICE MAY
HAVE SHARP TURNS, DETOURS, AND DISTRACTIONS,
YET IT IS ALWAYS THE SHORTEST ROUTE.

Although it may sound as if the people who were most influ-
ential in my spiritual journey were all men, that is not the
case. Among the people I met at the Nashville Buddhist Temple,
I got to know Jim best because we lived near each other, but
Carole also made a lasting impression on me, even though we
had less contact. Most important in my life at that time was
Jane, a psychologist. I had heard about her from a friend, who
related how in a therapists' training group, when everyone
named the one thing that held the greatest value for them, Jane
said, "the dharma," then had to explain what it meant.

I was intrigued. Since I had given up sitting at the Zen
Center, it occurred to me that I might enter therapy with
someone who knew about meditation and could guide me in
the right direction. I had asked around about therapists who
were involved in spiritual practice or knew about meditation,
and the only name I got was Jane's. I called her, and she agreed
to see me. Each week I took two buses to get to her house,
where I spent my fifty minutes in her living room with one or
another of her three cats in my lap.

The truth is that my life was a bit of a mess. I had impulsively left an East Coast city, a job, and a man to travel in

India, and when I returned, I had just as impulsively moved to the Midwest and started all over. I often told myself that what I wanted was a spiritual teacher, but, in fact, at the time therapy with Jane seemed to be what I needed.

Jane was deeply grounded in Buddhist practice. From the time of her first encounter with Buddhism, the dharma had illuminated all the dark, knotty questions of human suffering that had troubled her since childhood. Buddhism is about living intelligently, she said, not about being a nice person—not about anything other than exactly *what is*. Buddhist practice felt consistent with her work as a therapist. Indeed, for Jane, her practice and her work had become inseparably intertwined in a single process of being present to whatever arose in each moment. The process was ongoing and never ending, and truth was discerned at ever-deeper levels. That, Jane told me, was the meaning of *gate gate paragate parasamgate*:

> *Gone, gone*
> *Gone beyond*
> *Beyond beyond.*

Jane was motherly in the best sense, allowing me to feel unconditionally safe with her and yet asking of me that I be adult, responsible, reasonable, smart, kind, my best self. She was not only thoughtful and honest but also literate and witty, and she seemed to love me. At that time, those qualities added up to my picture of a perfect person. Now I can see that it looks more like a person on a pedestal.

Occasionally, I made efforts to draw Jane into the role of spiritual teacher. She was adamant that she could not be that for me, but she encouraged my interest in learning meditation. She also suggested that I contemplate an idea she had found helpful: *In Buddhism, you become a mother to yourself.* I liked the suggestion of comfort and safety, the ultimate in refuge. But it was a long time before I grasped the responsibility implied in those words, and how that very responsibility becomes a living practice.

✧   ✧   ✧

After the retreat in Nashville, Carole and I had exchanged a few letters. In one she enclosed a photocopied picture of U Pandita. He was younger and thinner and wore even heavier black-framed glasses and a blank expression. I pored over it, wondering why she had sent it and why I found it so intriguing.

I also thought about Achan Sobin and my undefined feelings toward him. I had told Achan that I would write and let him know how my meditation was going, but I never did. Sad to say, I let my spontaneous response to his goodness be forced aside by my conviction that I was spiritually lacking.

I was still mulling over how to devote a stretch of time to learning meditation when an opportunity arose in the form of a telephone call from Min, announcing the return of U Pandita. Min estimated that the Nashville Buddhist Temple could accommodate fifty to a hundred people. With ample space for sleeping, eating, and meditating, he figured, the limiting factor was bathroom facilities. Putting portable toilets in the roofless part of the building would solve that problem: indoor outhouses, Min called them happily.

I liked the idea of being at the temple again but was wary about sitting another Asian-style retreat. In my fantasies of the upcoming event, I saw myself as one of the smiling, gliding, whispering hostess team, preparing delectable dishes and doing whatever else was needed to serve the noble cause of the meditators. I did not see myself sitting. I had been a member of that noble team once, and once was enough.

Meanwhile, my summer headed off in a different direction, and I put the Buddhist Temple out of my mind. A chance meeting with Steven from U Pandita's first Nashville retreat led to my participating in a summer colloquium in New England. The colloquium, on religion and intellectual life, brought together twenty-five Protestants, Catholics, and Jews working on individual research projects. At Steven's suggestion, I decided to investigate the relation between Buddhist meditation and the branch of philosophy known as phenomenology. The phenomenologists, Steven said, especially Heidegger, sounded for all the world as if they were describing vipassana meditation.

Suddenly, sitting in a library and reading about philosophy—something in which I'd never had the slightest interest—seemed like the most fulfilling thing I could do with my life. I suspect I was trying to find intellectual justification for what I felt drawn to, trying to dress up the mysterious awe I felt toward U Pandita, the sweet affection for Achan Sobin, with something I believed to be more substantial than my own emotion. But I was conscious mainly of my desire to dive back into the familiar world of lines of type on pages of paper—the *answers*, surely, lay somewhere in all those books—rather than in pushing further into the formless unknown of meditation.

My experience of the colloquium was, in fact, the opposite of meditation. It was a banquet of books and ideas, a feast of words and concepts, a verbal binge—a final fling, as it turned out, with intellectual life. There were pages, volumes, whole libraries of words; our eyes, ears, and mouths were filled with them. During the day, working on my topic, I encountered my colleagues everywhere in pursuit of the Word, stalking their quarry in the library stacks, perusing the card catalog and microfiche index, lined up at the photocopy machine, sunk among piles of books in the library reading room. At 6:00, a great swell of talk arose over dinner, and evenings were given to formal presentations by members, which we then discussed, often late into the night.

I read enough to see the similarities between phenomenology and meditation. Both address human alienation from the world and from ourselves, and both are said to lead to a nondualistic understanding of the profound relatedness of all existence. Both offer a method rather than a belief system, and the method is based on direct examination of experience. As Jim had said to me, it's something you *do*. At that point, however, the philosophical texts became vague. I concluded that some rare individuals hack their way out of the jungle of subject-object dichotomy and live to tell of emerging into the clearing, so to speak, of nondualism. But describing the view at the end must be a lot easier than outlining step-by-step how they got there. Indeed, the systematic descriptions of the process in phenomenology are notoriously inscrutable. I could not imagine anyone but a philosopher plunging much further into those depths.

When a Catholic nun in the group reported on her study of Thomas Merton's writings, I was intrigued. I found a book of Merton's journals at the library and read from it each night before I went to sleep. The parts about vows and prayer and devotion and sacraments had no more connection to my life than philosophy did. But the parts about weather and work, plants and animals, seasons and sickness, doubt and longing, silence and solitude and joy evoked a life rich not so much with "meaning"—which was beginning to seem the least of it—but with beauty and love and, yes, pleasure. It was the very dailiness of the journal that touched me; what Merton wrote about sounded like something I already knew about, something I had already lived but could not quite remember. The life described in those journals was the life I wanted.

I was using as a bookmark one of the "Way of Mindfulness" flyers from Achan Sobin's retreat, and each night I reread from it his words:

*As a novice, I carefully applied myself to the study of
Buddhist teachings, scriptures, and history. I could
talk about abstruse points of philosophy and lecture on
meditation. My mind was packed with facts. Only
when I decided to put the books away and actually
entered meditation training myself did I begin to
understand what I had studied and what I had taught.*

Several of the colloquium participants were Quakers, and
we met each day to meditate together. The silence was a welcome refuge from our submersion in the flood of printed and
spoken communication, a little island of blessed emptiness onto
which we pulled ourselves each morning for a brief respite
before pushing off again into deep conceptual waters.

Sitting in silence was the most satisfying part of my day,
the most relevant things I read were by a Christian monk, and
a Buddhist monk was telling me to put the books away. What
all this meant, I scarcely dared to wonder.

On the Fourth of July, the Quakers and I went to a peace
march celebrating "interdependence." It was led by a Japanese
monk and two American Buddhist nuns, followed by a motley
contingent beating fanlike drums and chanting in Japanese. We
ended our walk near a Revolutionary War monument, where
we sat in a circle and sang "We Shall Overcome" and "This
Little Light of Mine" and songs in Latin and in Hebrew and in
a Native American language.

The Japanese monk stood apart from the group, across the
circle from me. His arms folded, his eyes half closed, he stood as
motionless as a statue, it seemed, amid the trailing branches of a
weeping willow. I watched him for a long time. Now and then
a breeze blew the willow branches gently back and forth in
front of him. Without moving his body or shifting his gaze or in
any way unsettling that perfect stillness, each time a branch
brushed past his face, he gently put his lips out to meet it.

✧ ✧ ✧

By the time I returned from the colloquium, I had decided to leave my job. Jane agreed that more reading and studying would not take me where I wanted to go, that I needed someone to translate arcane language into living practice, a teacher who could make the connection to my life. I felt that some path was out there for me, somewhere, if only I could get directions to it.

Every time I saw in my mind's eye the Japanese monk standing so, so still and moving his lips to kiss the willow, I knew that he knew something I did not know, something I couldn't imagine an American knowing. On the other hand, if I wanted to address the deep problems of my character—my near-terminal restlessness, say—surely it would be easier to deal with someone from my own culture.

I wrote to Southern Dharma, asking if it would be possible to spend an extended period there. That way, I figured, I could observe various teachers who came to lead retreats and see if any of them felt right for me. I received a letter back from a woman named Anna, one of the founders, saying that they accepted individual retreatants and also that they were looking for staff. She suggested that I come for a few days, see how I liked it, and talk with her about what I was interested in. We set a date for a few weeks away.

✧ ✧ ✧

I had another reason for wanting to leave where I was, but it was not something I could admit to at the time. Fundamentally, it was the same old reason that had, unacknowledged, driven my life, pushing me from one place to the next, one person to another. It's the same force, in fact, that drives all of us: in a word, discomfort—psychic, not physical, discomfort, but on the path of meditation, you quickly learn that they essentially boil down to the same thing. Knee hurts? Shift position. Now back hurts? Shift again. Hand itches? Scratch. Knee hurts again? Move. At the end of thirty minutes, most of what has happened is discomfort and lots of moving around, while you have worn into deeper ruts the illusion that your reactions control your experience. You have no center from which to observe, to learn, to choose intelligent actions over illusory ones. No ground from which to develop the strength and resilience that comes only in stillness.

In the same way, life presents all sorts of psychic discomforts. Uncentered, ungrounded, one responds according to one's personality and one's conditioned patterns of behavior. Don't like your job? There's always getting angry about it. Or there's staying put and hating the boss and allowing that hatred to harden into part of your identity. Or there's running away and starting over. Someone doesn't like you? You can let them know how wrong and stupid they are, settling the matter once and for all. Or you can indulge in the internal back and forth of itemizing their faults and then picking over your own. Or you can run away and start over with better, smarter, more sensitive and appreciative people. Things just generally not working out? You don't have what you want, or you have it and now it's not enough, or it's fine but *you* are not enough? You can blame the world, you can make excuses, or you can run away to that promised land where everything will be exactly as you want it, always and forever.

The third option had always been my first choice.

Jane, my surrogate mother figure, a placid, settled person who had always lived in the same place, helped me not only to see that pattern in myself but also to acknowledge its destructiveness. In feeble defense, I invoked the Buddhist idea that freedom lies in not clinging to anything, since everything changes—of always going beyond, beyond beyond. Was I not a soaring free spirit, unattached to the conventional possessions and roles that doom most people to lives of dreary sameness? Was I not a living example of "letting go"?

"No," Jane said. "You are not. You cannot let go of something you have never had."

The challenge for me, she said decisively, was to acquire things and to let the caring for them—people, pets, house, yard, car, clothes, furniture—bring ballast to my life, binding me enough that I could settle, stay put, and learn what can only be learned in the process of sticking it out through the discomfort.

I could understand the wisdom in that, but I was not aware that I was still seeing it through my own filter. My vision of a stable life tacitly featured Jane at the center, a deeply grounded, maternal maypole around which my life would gaily whirl. Jane would patiently disentangle me from life's messiness when I ran too fast or stumbled or thrashed around, heedlessly wreaking damage and destruction.

Already, with Jane's encouragement, I had acquired a steady job and my first car. Before I had time to rest in my settledness, however, the ground shifted under me. For the first time in my life, I was the one who got left, when Jane notified me that she was ending my therapy.

I begged her to tell me what I could do so that she would reconsider. In response, I received a long handwritten letter explaining her point of view, accepting responsibility, but reiterating her decision not to work with me. I was incredulous, outraged, shaken. I wanted to defend myself against what I took to be accusations, yet I could not grasp what the problem was. What could be so awful about me that the one person devoted to helping had abandoned the effort? I carried Jane's letter around with me and reread it many times. Continuing my life in the same way seemed impossible, and I took the whole devastating incident as a sign pointing toward a completely new direction, a new start. Again.

✦ ✦ ✦

Since Nashville was on my way to Southern Dharma, I called Min. He invited me to stay overnight at the Buddhist Temple and to have dinner with him at the Thai restaurant so he could tell me about U Pandita's second visit, which had been another success.

On my way to the restaurant, I stopped to see the Nashville replica of the Parthenon. It is shockingly intact, compared, at least, with the familiar images of the Acropolis in our minds and books and posters and art history slides. Indeed, the very substantiality of the Nashville version, it struck me then, is incongruous when you consider those great ideas associated with the cultural legacy of the Greeks: Logic, Rationality, Balance, and Order, indeed, Western Civilization itself—all rather worn and tattered now and coming apart at the seams. The march of metopes around the top, each little sculptured scene as full and fresh as if it were carved yesterday, has the precision and regularity of a military drill, the alternating square panels measuring space and time into one-two, left-right, subject-object, East-is-East-and-West-is-West duality, as if that way of things were fixed forever.

But looking at the great, godlike figures of the pediment, the prototypical heroes of our culture, with their great European high-bridged noses and energized bodies and blank eyes, trying halfheartedly to recall what I once knew about them (whatever it is one says when lecturing about the Parthenon), I could think only of U Pandita. He was the opposite—at rest, immobile, blank, but with very alive eyes. Like statues of the Buddha.

Over supper, Min recounted the high points of U Pandita's second visit. More boys had been ordained, and more Americans had come to learn meditation, including several from the first retreat. Carole had demonstrated remarkable progress, which pleased the Sayadaw. On the other hand, the temple faced serious problems. One of the monks had returned to Burma, leaving only two, and the building was in worse disrepair than ever.

When I got to the temple that night, a scrawny young monk let me in, nodding and smiling and looking at the floor. I said I remembered him from the first retreat with U Pandita. Yes, yes, he smiled, and motioned me into the office. We struggled to talk, then U Jotipala, the abbot, arrived and presented me with copies of sermons and teachings he had delivered at the temple. I sensed that the monks were starved for company.

One of U Jotipala's sermons was entitled "The Nature of Our Body" and seemed to speak to the general theme of the flesh being weak. Another, entitled "The Power of the Fire of Lust," began: *The fire of lust is hotter than the fire of the world. The one who has the experience of burning on the fire of lust can clearly understand the profound meaning of this sentence. So, the Buddha concisely said, "There is no fire like lust."*

I woke up the next morning weighed down with a sadder-but-wiser feeling at the unexpected humanness I perceived in the monks' situation. Or, it occurred to me, my own situation. Were we all lost souls? What did I really know about the monks? Almost nothing. What did I really know about myself?

When I was ready to leave, U Jotipala followed me outside. He peered into the car as I opened the door.

"Car is like house," he said, laughing.

I could not imagine U Jotipala looking with envy on my possessions or my car or even a house. My freedom, though, to take it all or leave it, to go where I pleased—I imagined that he might envy that, and, were such freedom given to him, that he would head straight home to Burma. Homesick monks. It did not seem right, did not match my notion of selfless surrender to a higher calling. But there it was—in my mind, at least.

Now I wonder, could it be that homesickness was something I found so unbearable that I displaced it onto them?

At the time, I was completely caught up in the opposite of homesickness, the need to leave my old life behind, to go somewhere new. As I pulled away from the temple, wound past a couple of blocks of housing projects, then zipped into the traffic on the interstate, my mind was already at the next new place. Southern Dharma.

And, if I did not like it there, another possibility existed, another next new place: I could come live in the temple in exchange for work. I would have my sleeping bag and towel and clothes in the room across from the meditation hall, away from the monks, and I would eat rice soup in the morning and whatever they had for lunch and go to the Thai restaurant or get a pizza now and then in the evening. I would meditate twice a day and maybe keep silence.

Mostly, though, I would work. Get rid of the tree-of-paradise saplings growing from cracks and next to the walls of the building. Clean debris from the front steps. Plant some evergreens and low-maintenance perennials. And in the back, a vegetable garden.

As for the altars—I would leave them untouched. There was something precious in their being just what they were.

I let the fantasy run for fifty miles or so. It had the intensity of lust and began to exhaust me. I switched on the radio and sang along with Glen Campbell, "Gentle on My Mind."

✥ ✥ ✥

The aura of specialness around the temple faded with time, as it does in love affairs. What was wholly wonderful becomes sad and wonderful, and finally just sad and sort of quaint. On later trips through Nashville, passing by on the interstate, I wondered how much of my fascination with that place, that little hidden world, lay in the implicit promise of those years when I read books about spiritual life, traveled in India, and sought out Asian meditation teachers.

Now the temple stands in my memory alongside other places and people and things that became the objects of inordinate passion, things that I wanted to save or that I wanted to have save me. In the case of the Buddhist Temple, it was some of both, salvage and salvation. What keeps it alive for me is the seductive beauty in its very unlikeliness, the possibility that beckons within the improbable.

THE LAST RESORT

IN SILENCE: SITTING MEDITATION

No one ever dies of restlessness, meditation teachers like to say, but people like me suspect people like them of being innately calm. What could they know of our agonies?

In the first two sittings today, as restlessness reached a high pitch, I had moments of thinking I might die. Normally, the melodramas that take place in silent sitting are all internal; the most that happens externally is that somebody coughs or a branch clatters onto the roof or a bug crawls along the wall where your gaze is fixed. But this morning, the teacher did two things that shifted my attention away from myself and broke my escalating fear of boredom.

During the first sitting, in the middle of the silence, from the direction of the teacher's cushion came an astonishingly loud clap, a single sharp report, like a gunshot. I felt all the minds in the room converge in a one-pointed question: What did it mean? After some minutes of intense wondering, I resigned myself to the probability that I would never know and sank back into my separate world of thought.

In the next sitting, I heard a rustling from the teacher's cushion then the swish of a long, heavy robe moving toward a window where a wasp buzzed. Clink of little brass bell on the glass, muffling the buzz, then the sound of paper slid between glass and bell, then the swish of robe moving to the door. Sneaking a quick look behind me, I saw the teacher release the wasp outside.

Now we are sitting on our cushions waiting for the teacher to begin the nightly discussion.

Waiting.

Waiting.

Waiting.

"What would you like to talk about?" The teacher's words are so soft they hardly break the silence, yet they are crystal clear.

In the soft glow of the rice-paper lamps around the walls, the stark triangle of the teacher's black robe looks flat, timeless, empty, while the head surmounting it is intensely alive—motionless, but radiant with energy, color, blood, nerve, bone, muscle, being. Now that words have been spoken, a question asked, something is bound to follow. We will talk. Restlessness dissolves.

✦ ✦ ✦

When I think back on retreats, I always remember them as wonderful. This is an odd thing to say, since any retreat entails such suffering: prolonged physical discomfort;

tedium intensified to agonizing degrees; uncommon restrictions and frustrations; strong doses of doubt, self-loathing, fear, the gamut of negative emotions; the conviction that your wretchedness is far worse than anyone else's; and a generalized misery born from the combination of these things. But the good parts are indescribably fine. Small signs of progress, like finding how to sit on the edge of the cushion so that your back and hips come into an easy natural alignment and you are completely comfortable. The relief of tears when you let go the hardness of your heart and open to your suffering. Heavenly periods of stillness and peace. The incredible expansion of your perception and the resulting appreciation of beauty in the simplest things. Being flooded with gratitude and wonder and love. Timeless instants of liberation from the incessant strain of being somebody. And laughing together during the discussions—laughter like no other, inexplicable, uproarious, deep, full, free, rocking the beams of the meditation hall, and, I imagine, resounding outward from our mountainside to fill the universe.

CHAPTER 5

A PATH IN THE WILDERNESS

ALONG WITH EXPECTATIONS COME DOUBTS.
LIFE ROLLS ON, REGARDLESS.

Southern Dharma is high in the Blue Ridge Mountains of west-ern North Carolina. It is at the end of a tortuous climb up a marginal road, a long way from the last habitation, immeasurably distant from the world of deadlines, achievement, hyperactivity. Whenever I think of it, a moment of stillness opens in my heart.

In its largest meaning, *dharma* means "law," in the sense of natural law, how things are. In Buddhism, it specifically refers to the spiritual teaching and practice. The hint of incongruity in the name "Southern Dharma" amused me; in the early 1980s, the southeastern United States was largely a dharma-free zone, at least in the narrow sense of the word. Anna had told me, when we talked by phone, that when she and a friend decided to start a retreat center, they wanted it to be where it was most needed, so they put it right in the middle of the South. For me, that deci-sion was a piece of good fortune; the South was known and com-fortable, a safe place in which to pursue such a seemingly foreign practice as meditation.

Southern Dharma also provided an escape, but I didn't want to think about that. Going there meant I wouldn't have to do a second retreat with Achan Sobin, which was in the works, nor would I have to act on my fantasy about living and working at the Buddhist Temple. And I could avoid facing at least some of the pain of being rejected by Jane; in a new place, no one would know about it. The excitement of starting over somewhere else would overwrite those abortive chapters of my life. And if anything was known and comfortable, it was the pattern of leaving and starting over.

✧ ✧ ✧

It was late fall in the mid-1980s when I went to Southern Dharma for the first time. The brightest of the autumn color was gone, and so were the tourists who flocked to the mountains to see it. I remember driving fast through the sparsely settled valley, wondering if the local people were happy to be left alone with the season's final, more subtle display. For me, the lingering yellow of the poplars, catching the sun in shimmers of pale gold up the mountainsides, gleamed with promise.

The directions Anna had given me said to take the blacktop through the valley for six miles, and at the green dumpster, to turn right onto the bridge over the stream, then follow the gravel road about a mile to a group of mailboxes. She warned me that the next mile, from the mailboxes up to the top of the ridge, seems farther than it is but not to worry because you can't get lost. Once you head down the other side into the cove, there's nowhere else to go, she said. Southern Dharma is the end of the road.

At the mailboxes, the road turned to clay tracks, ran through a shallow stream, then narrowed and rose abruptly. The first two turns were so steep and sharp that I took them only after several tries. I drove in low gear, moving slowly around the switchbacks through fluttering, drifting leaves, dark pines, looming boulders, deepening stillness. It was a long way. The road wound up and up and up, back and forth across the mountainside. Feeling lost, but going on, because there was no place to turn around.

Finally, with immense relief, I reached the top of the ridge. As the road turned down along the steep side of a cove, something just below the banked clay shoulder caught my eye. I stopped to look. It was the ruins of a log cabin, a heap of moss- and vine-covered timbers sunk into the shadowed hillside. A comparatively permanent reminder of impermanence, I thought, nature's silent memento mori, appropriately situated at the start of the descent into this place dedicated to contemplation.

Slowly, slowly, I followed the twisting ruts into the cove, emerging from the deep woods at the edge of a clearing. Beyond a tall boxwood hedge stood another abandoned dwelling, this one stark with recent loss—the freshly charred debris of a house burned to the ground. The Second Sign of Impermanence. I stopped again and got out of my car. Through my mind passed the biblical saying about losing everything in order to gain it. I stared at the remains of the house: the lifeless ebony sheen of crumpled timbers, scattered sheets of tin roofing, the soot-smeared brick chimney, ashes—everything gone. Holding my breath against the fumes of damped fire and old smoke, I felt a wave of dread.

I considered escaping back down the mountain, but the clearing seemed to hold me. I stood at one edge of the bowl of space that opened up and out from the brown meadow on either side of the road to the woods beyond, and on to the distant gray-blue mountain ridges, to the clouds drifting up from the valley, to the sky. It was too late to turn and leave. Claimed by some gentle force field, I was hopelessly at home in an utterly strange place.

A stream splashed over a pile of boulders behind the burned house, then burbled under a stone bridge and along the edge between meadow and woods. In the middle of the clearing, a rough trapezoid of posts and wires marked a garden, empty except for a few dead sunflowers leaning against one another with their giant heads looking down at the earth. Among scattered apple trees were beehives, a decrepit barn, and a shed filled with neat stacks of firewood. Across the clearing, the road disappeared again into trees, through which the clean lines of a new building were visible.

Tires crunched softly in the distance. I looked back the way I had come to glimpse an orange truck rounding the switchbacks. Slowly, slowly it descended into the cove, a big, boxy old pickup. It stopped behind my car, and a woman stepped out and greeted me.

Anna's soft, husky voice was perfect for the place, a blend of southern warmth and dharma cool. Her gold-and-silver looks—light blue eyes and white-blond curls poking out around the band of a corduroy cap—were more like my idea of an angel than of someone who had hacked this space out of the wilderness to build a retreat center.

I asked about the house that had burned down. It was an old farmhouse, Anna said, and she had lived there. All her belongings were lost in the fire, along with her four cats, the journals she had kept for many years, and photographs documenting the building of the retreat center. She showed me how the boxwood hedge was scorched where it had faced the flames.

"I try not to fall into thinking it was meant to teach me about nonattachment," she said. "It just happened."

We drove across the clearing and parked, then Anna showed me through the main building. The ground floor housed a dining room, a kitchen, an office, and a library. The second floor was a dormitory, and the third was a sleeping loft. The spaces were plainly but beautifully designed, and the construction, which used local wood, was sturdy and handsome.

From the second floor, we followed a short path around the curve of the mountainside to the meditation hall. One side of the building was set against the steep slope, facing into a mass of bushes and vines; the other hung in space among the tops of trees. A wide roofed porch wrapped around all four sides.

"This," Anna said, "is the heart of the place."

Inside, the walls were plain white, the wooden floor bare. Windows on the side walls and three long skylights in the southern slope of the roof admitted a pale light, and small round stained-glass windows were set high in each of the end walls. The room was empty except for meditation cushions and mats stacked along the back wall, a woodstove at one side, a low wooden platform in the front, and behind it, against the wall, where an altar would be, a narrow low table. The table had nothing on it, and I smiled to myself, thinking of the exuberant altars at the Buddhist Temple.

On that first visit, I stayed in a cabin used for solitary retreats. A ten-minute walk out a trail from the main building, the cabin was a single room built of rough lumber and roofed with corrugated metal. It opened directly onto the downhill side of the trail, and its back corners were supported by wooden beams planted in the steep slope. The vertical plank siding was not sawed off evenly at the floor line but extended beyond it in an irregular, snaggle-toothed pattern. I liked that; it matched my idea of rustic simplicity.

Inside the cabin, however, coziness had run rampant. A double bed was neatly made up with blue flannel sheets and a blue paisley comforter. There were ruffled curtains at the windows, a woodstove, a washbasin, soap, and two jugs of water. On a bedside table were a kerosene lantern, matches, a mug, a book of poems, a pencil, and a notepad—everything you would need and some extra things you just might like to have. Somebody had put a lot of care into the place.

Next to the lantern was a page of typed instructions: safety precautions, warnings about distinguishing between water for drinking and water for bathing, requests to conserve water and wood, detailed procedures for cleaning the cabin before leaving. Clipped to the instruction sheet was a separate paragraph on the subject of toothbrushing. Toothpaste should not be spit out the door, nor should water into which toothpaste had been spat be tossed down the hillside, leaving a conspicuous white trace, which would be unsightly for people who walk by on the trail. Toothpaste should be disposed of by rinsing the washbasin in enough water (but not too much) to dilute it, then dumped mindfully. I wondered how long it would take me to master the technique of brushing my teeth without leaving a trace, and if spiritual progress could be measured by such accomplishments.

Anna heated some soup for supper, and after we had eaten, she gave me a flashlight for the walk to the cabin. As I left the main building behind, the flashlight's wan circle of light seemed very small. I swung it back and forth, trying to see more of what I was walking toward, but beyond the edge of light was always more unknown. I was afraid, partly of what dangers might lurk (I had in mind laggard snakes who had not yet made it into hibernation). But mostly I feared that the searching beam of light would betray my nervousness, should Anna be looking in my direction.

I stopped and turned off the flashlight. I had walked in the dark before, I reminded myself. I took a few tentative steps. My fear vanished. I realized that the light itself, or rather my dependence on it, was what made me think I could know what was ahead, and that belief created an illusion of being in control. Against that expectation, the looming darkness was intolerable. If, however, *all* of it was unknown, there was nothing to do but accept that and keep going. By the time I reached the cabin, I was at ease in the night wilderness. I did not bother to light the lantern, but undressed and felt my way into bed in the dark.

During the days I was at Southern Dharma, my attention was mostly focused on the place itself. Anna and I met at the meditation hall twice a day and sat in silence for half an hour. At mealtimes, she prepared food, and we cleaned up together afterward. I spent one morning gathering kindling and stacking firewood that Anna had cut from a fallen tree. Otherwise, I was on my own.

One afternoon, I walked through dense forest to the top of the mountain, a grassy bald rising among rolling meadows and magnificent old trees. From the panoramic view of the mountains to the small herd of cows grazing nearby, everything spelled peace and perfection. If only I could spend time in that spot, say, once a week, as a sort of Sabbath ritual, going to the top of the mountain might—who knows?—bring greater spiritual benefit than hours of sitting meditation could. The place itself seemed enough for me. Retreats and teachers and meditation techniques paled in comparison to being in the environment of calm, quiet, and simplicity. Southern Dharma felt like a path that opened in the wilderness of my yearning.

When I talked with Anna about returning for a longer period, she suggested that I come in the early spring when they would be needing a staff member to assist the manager who was being hired. The center was closed for the first two months of the year, and March would be spent getting it ready for retreats, which began in April. If I came for those two months, Anna said, I could see what it was like to work there during the off-season, and then I would have a chance to meet teachers who came to lead retreats.

I was thrilled. Back in the Midwest, the next few months passed quickly, as I spent the winter arranging to move my life elsewhere for a while. At the end of February, I was on my way back to Southern Dharma.

Driving into the cove again, I caught myself feeling like a pilgrim. There was the ruined log cabin, and then, where the road enters the clearing, the site of the burned farmhouse. I stopped to look. Winter had scoured away most of the remains.

Only the chimney stood, a bare, cold, lonely relic, and there were still some blackened places on the ground. But already fragrant new growth burgeoned inside the boxwood hedge.

✧ ✧ ✧

I went to work at Southern Dharma with many of the common misconceptions about spiritual life: that it is best cultivated in a sacred sort of place, preferably a secluded one. That if I just tried hard enough for a certain period—say, a year—I would attain a state of effortless and enduring bliss.

Along with my great expectations, I entertained great doubts—mainly that I was not the spiritual type and that any endeavors in that line were doomed to failure. On the other hand, I would tell myself, I am not expecting total enlightenment, I just want to learn to meditate. Meditation, I was convinced, would smooth into place the ragged pieces of my life, and then I would be happy. All I needed was a way to live on this side of enlightenment. Nirvana could be postponed for another lifetime.

When I arrived, Joel, the new manager, was in the kitchen, tending an impressive alfalfa and mung bean sprouting operation. He had Anna's angelic coloring in stronger tones, his wavy hair darker gold, his eyes brighter blue. Working at retreat centers was a career path that suited him, Joel said, his eyes twinkling. He had worked at several, most recently as a macrobiotic cook, and he had met many well-known spiritual teachers. One of the advantages of living at a place like Southern Dharma, he said, is getting to know the teachers who come through. He thought I was probably ready to meet my teacher. That sounded a little too much like "meet my Maker," and I dismissed it as the type of vague mystical notion you hear from the type of people who work at retreat centers.

Joel's devotion to the spiritual path was all embracing. The dashboard of his truck reminded me of the South Asian more-is-more altar at the Buddhist Temple; it was decked out like a shrine with pictures of Ram Dass's guru Maharaji wrapped in his plaid blanket, smiling sly and sweet from his grizzled three-day beard; the young Meher Baba, transported by bliss; and the Virgin Mary standing in a crescent moon against a starry firmament. My own notions, I observed, were lighter on the mystic and heavier on the monastic.

The retreat center was a bit of a disappointment in that regard. Except for the quiet and solitude, the only thing about the place that could be construed as even faintly monastic was the spareness of the dormitory. Each room had a small table and two wooden bunk beds with space underneath for drawers. Because the drawers had not been built yet, the natural thing was to keep your belongings on the bed you were not sleeping in, or on both beds. Confronting this display every time I entered my room, I noticed that sometimes it seemed to reproach me with the undeniable fact that even the few possessions I allowed myself to bring far exceeded my needs, while at other times I congratulated myself on how simply I lived. Likewise, the arrangement of the items suggested my uncontrollable disorderliness, or, alternatively, my innate sense of proper placement.

These debates about the True Me were never resolved, and I attempted to impose some consistency on the situation by keeping my towel neatly folded on its rack and my toothbrush and toothpaste meticulously centered on their tiny shelf. On the wall above the shelf was a postcard-sized mirror mounted at the level of my throat. I prided myself on never stooping to look in it, believing that discipline was important in principle and that any renunciation of vanity was for the good. Personal adornments, of course, I had left at home.

During the first month, Anna was there off and on, but mostly it was just Joel and me. I considered Joel truly spiritual because he never got angry, he smiled a lot, he always took a positive attitude toward difficulties, and he played tapes of dharma talks by various teachers while he worked in the kitchen. On the other hand, there were things I disapproved of, for example, the mountain of gear in Joel's room, which appeared to be one of everything sold by Recreational Equipment, Inc., plus an awesome number of tape cassettes.

At the time, I was unaware of being trapped in the dualities of constant judgment—this is good/that is bad—and unaware that each side of the duality necessarily implies the other. I thought my judgments meant I was getting somewhere, figuring things out. Yes, Joel is a spiritual sort of person, but, no, Joel isn't entirely clear about material possessions. I did not notice how readily my judgments shifted and even contradicted themselves and how the little burst of satisfaction that accompanied judgment faded almost immediately. Nor did I notice that in judging, my attention was focused entirely outside myself, that my sense of who I was and what I was doing was based on external comparisons: what Joel was/wasn't, what Southern Dharma was/wasn't, what I should be according to all sorts of unquestioned assumptions.

I didn't notice because I had not yet turned my attention to my own mind. Not looking at myself in the mirror was like not looking inward, in that both were based on a mistaken idea about the nature of ego and the spiritual path. Genuine interest in oneself is crucial to spiritual growth; the process of self-examination is how one gains deeper knowledge and ultimately wisdom. In the words of the Zen master Dogen, *To study the dharma is to study the self. To study the self is to forget the self. To forget the self is to be enlightened by all things.*

The fact was that I quickly became much more interested in work than in spiritual practice. I had envisioned being outdoors most of the time, putting in a garden, building a compost heap, chop-wood-carry-water sorts of things that had seeped into my awareness from reading about monastic life. But to my dismay, the work to be done was mostly desk work: correspondence, bookkeeping, publicity, program development, the basics for a small nonprofit organization.

The office was a narrow sun room off the kitchen, occupied by plastic tubs of sprouts and a new cat Anna had taken in, who snoozed in a box of brochures. I could tell that the space would feel confining to me. My mind leapt around to other possibilities for more meaningful work, but what needed doing at Southern Dharma wasn't nearly as obvious as it had been at the Buddhist Temple. Brand new, well designed and constructed, set in the middle of a mountain forest, the retreat center couldn't have been more different from the temple near the interstate; certainly, it needed nothing in the way of landscaping or restoration or sprucing up. Only two small projects occurred to me: establishing a compost heap and putting flowers in the meditation hall.

During my first weekend at Southern Dharma I did no work at all. Joel had not had time to plan jobs for me and had gone off backpacking with his son, Ryan, who had come for a visit. Anna was away too. I sat around in the kitchen, where a sort of satellite office had grown up with a small desk squeezed between the freezer and the backdoor. On the desk next to the telephone and answering machine were some note pads, but, I noticed, nothing to write with. Maybe I could introduce a higher level of efficiency and professionalism to this operation, I thought. But I put that impulse aside. It had raised in me a vaguely sensed tension I associated with feeling driven about work. That tension was all too familiar, and I was at Southern Dharma to look for something different.

I wandered into the library and glanced through magazines on spiritual life. I felt uncomfortable about not being productive and worried that the place might burn down while I was the only one there. I did not even consider filling the time with meditation.

✧ ✧ ✧

There was a certain irony, I thought, in coming to Southern Dharma to further my spiritual growth by enduring the rigors of an austere lifestyle, then finding myself surrounded by material comforts.

"It's almost like a resort here," I said to Joel.

Joel just smiled, but he, too, must have felt the need for something closer to nature, because he and Ryan decided to "camp out" in the cabin. I told them about the flashlight epiphany I had had when I stayed there.

During the night, I heard soft footsteps coming up the dormitory stairs, then Ryan's voice and Joel's whisper, then the door closing to their room down the hall. The next morning when I came into the kitchen, Joel was ladling out bowls of buckwheat groats from a huge pot.

I asked why they hadn't stayed at the cabin. Ryan said they had heard noises and could not sleep, so came back to spend the rest of the night in the dorm.

"There was a snake under the roof," Ryan said. Joel gave him a look, and he amended his assertion. "Not last night, but another time, when somebody else was sleeping there. They told my dad."

Joel touched the boy's arm. "It's okay to be scared. And it's okay to let Sara know we were scared. She was scared, too, walking out there by herself."

"But . . . but later she wasn't scared. And she stayed out there all night."

"I was so worried about not leaving toothpaste in the bushes that I wouldn't have noticed snakes in the roof," I said. "But I won't be sleeping out there again, now that I do know about them."

Joel sprinkled his cereal with sunflower seeds and passed them to me. "Anyway, if Sara stays here long enough, she'll have a chance to confront being scared even if she doesn't sleep in the cabin. Not of snakes, maybe, but whatever she's afraid of in herself. That's what people come here for, Ryan, did you know that? They want to learn to look at their fear and make friends with it. Then, when they feel afraid, it doesn't bother them."

❖ ❖ ❖

When I asked Joel how often he went up to the top of the mountain, he rolled his eyes. There was never time for that sort of thing, he said. I wondered about that; it didn't seem accurate. But once we got into a routine of working hard day in and day out—my favorite routine, in fact—I forgot all about spending sacred time on the mountaintop.

Early morning and late afternoon, Joel and I and, when she was there, Anna, made our way along the gravel path and up the stepping-stones to the meditation hall. I spent much of my time on the cushion thinking of what I would do when the sitting was over, and sometimes my mind churned up emotion about where my life was going and what was wrong with me. Off the cushion, though, I gradually discovered something that felt far more real and significant: a clear, strong, deep experience of aloneness, as if I were settling into myself. I could not tell if it was the meditation or just the solitude and silence, but I became keenly aware of constant, subtle shifts in what was going on around me.

When I look back to that time, what I recall most vividly is how changes of temperature, moisture, wind, and light registered on the landscape. March washed the trees and rocks and ground and sky with frost, rain, and mists that blew up from the valley in damp, gray veils. By April, clusters of dogwood blossoms drifted like clouds through the woods. On bright days they looked like flotillas of butterflies; on dark days, scattered across the ink-wash ground of lichen-covered boulders, they looked as if they had been tossed into space by a Zen painter.

The chance to observe such beauty, and its continual passing away, was all the teaching I wanted. Sitting on a cushion and noticing my breath seemed superfluous, contrived, the long way round.

That initial euphoria, however, soon proved as transient as everything else. Familiar quandaries, frustrations, and general discontent regained their ground in my mind, and with a vengeance. My mental distress manifested physically in a sort of gasping breath and bouts of crying every time I sat in meditation. Miracles might be happening everywhere I turned my eyes, but once my attention was captured by my inner turmoil, it didn't matter. I was surrounded by heaven and living in hell.

❖   ❖   ❖

The habit of mindfulness, of paying attention, of simply being present to what is happening, requires practice: thus, meditation retreats. That April, Southern Dharma offered an introductory meditation retreat; a work-meditation retreat; a sesshin, eight days of intensive meditation; and, throughout the month, the guidance of a Zen teacher-in-residence.

The teacher's name was Cheri Huber. Cheri was from California, where people dabble in Eastern religion and then call themselves teachers. That was the sort of thing from which I had always intended to keep my distance.

As the day neared for the teacher's arrival, I developed overt pangs of anxiety. I told myself that they were simply due to my not wanting to change the comfortable routine Joel and I had settled into. I was clinging to the increasingly desperate hope that merely by submitting to the lifestyle of a retreat center, I would find some inner discipline automatically established, and

the pervasive calm virtue of the place would somehow transform me into whatever it was I wanted.

In fact, just being there *was* enough—not because of some
spiritual osmosis, but because in that place I encountered the
teacher who showed me that spiritual practice is right here,
right now, within me.

CHAPTER 6

MEETING THE TEACHER

**THE TEACHER IS BOTH ORDINARY AND EXTRAORDINARY,
AND SO ARE WE.**

The preparations for Cheri's stay were simple. Anna cleaned
one of the dormitory rooms and made up the bed, and Joel
drove down the mountain to a gas station and bought a case of
diet cola, the only special treatment Cheri requested.

When Cheri arrived, it was without fanfare, during the
night. I saw her first the next day in the kitchen. She looked
to be in her forties, about my age, and she was short, with pale
green eyes, ruddy cheeks, and straight gray hair cut close to her
head. She wore faded black sweatpants, an animal rights
T-shirt, and rather frumpy blue quilted bedroom slippers.
Standing there drinking a diet cola and showing around photographs of her grandson, she seemed ordinary enough.

What might give her away as a spiritual teacher? I wondered. How she stood and sat and moved, at once solid and
flexible, grounded yet incredibly light. Her eyes, which
seemed to have seen a lot and to be taking in everything, every
moment. The way she abandoned herself to laughter: her laugh
seemed to spring from some deep well of human connectedness,
gushing up out of her like a fountain, pouring forth as the most
natural response to the vagaries, ironies, incongruities, and
manifold absurdities of life.

Anna had told us that Cheri never gave formal dharma talks, the way most teachers do, but simply talked dharma all the time. Indeed, even in the most mundane conversation, she persistently nudged our awareness beyond habitual boundaries. Joel loved it. He asked endless questions, Anna asked a few, Cheri answered, and I listened. I must have listened very intently, because I could recall her words with astonishing clarity. I replayed them over and over, pondering the parts I found most baffling and pondering as well those that touched my heart, softened me, held some promise I scarcely dared think about.

The first of many such discussions took place that morning in the kitchen. What I remember of it is this.

Joel asked, "Would you say the point of meditation is learning to see clearly how things are?"

"Yes," Cheri said. "But we can't start seeing clearly until we drop some of our conditioned patterns of responding. Do you know what I mean by conditioning?"

"Beliefs about who we are, which come from childhood training and—"

"And are reinforced socially," Anna put in.

Cheri responded, "Beliefs about who we are, yes. We can be so focused on trying to make what we already believe fit into what's actually happening that there's no possibility of simply being present here and now. Zen practice is grounded in the understanding that you don't have to make what you believe—what you've been *conditioned* to believe—fit into what's happening. You can forget it, drop it, just be here right now, just be present to this moment."

I remember how her eyes fixed intently on Joel's, then Anna's, then mine.

"So," Joel said slowly, "the reason we practice is not to find something that can be applied universally, but to increase the number of moments we are fully aware?"

"That's one way to look at it," Cheri replied. "But a problem with quantifying is our tendency to slip into making it a
contest, competing with ourselves. I can see it now, little
charts on which we check off the number of moments of awareness in a day. And we count them up, thinking, 'Okay, now,
tomorrow, I'll do better, I'll get in more moments,' and next
thing we know, we're in a big struggle to beat our record.
Remember, this whole process of being aware only works one
moment at a time. This moment—oh, yes, I'll come back to the
present. And now, this moment.'"

She paused. The moments of silence that followed remain
vivid in my memory, as if she had literally given us those
moments so we could experience for ourselves what she was
talking about.

"And you can bring to each moment all the sincerity of
desire that you would bring to competing," she said softly.
"But with spiritual practice, it's concentrated in the present,
not dispersed in your memories of how you did yesterday, or
your expectations about the future, or any image of yourself."

Joel nodded.

Cheri's voice was hardly more than a whisper, but it was
clearly audible. "It's just this: right now, your whole heart
wanting to be right here."

✧ ✧ ✧

The day before the first retreat, Joel and Anna had an argument
about who was in charge of what tasks and who made deci-
sions. Nothing was resolved. Joel drove into Asheville to buy
food. Anna took the big orange truck down with a load of
gravel to repair rutted spots in the road.

Cheri looked at me and said, "Somebody's got to clean this
place. And I think it's going to be us."

She made a list of what needed to be done, and I got out cleaning supplies. While we mopped and vacuumed the floors and scrubbed the bathrooms, she chattered away.

"Do you know the purpose of the headlight on this vacuum cleaner?" she inquired, leaning over to examine the ancient contraption. "Vacuuming in the dark, maybe?"

I couldn't help laughing. But I was taken aback by the touch of frivolousness in her personality and by how, in the obvious ways, at least, she was not all that different from me. If I had stopped to question my assumptions, I would have seen that I had defined *myself* and *spiritual person* to be opposite and mutually exclusive terms. In spiritual endeavors, anyway, I was ordinary, and a Zen teacher, by definition, was extraordinary. I would not have said that I felt my capacity for spiritual attainment to be limited, but, in fact, my expectations were strictly boxed in by an unconscious belief based on "self" as compared to "other." There was "me," and outside me were "them," and the difference between us loomed large.

Cheri and I ended up outside the kitchen door, wringing out the mop and emptying the vacuum cleaner bag. The next thing I knew we were sitting on the step, and I was asking questions.

"How can you stand being in such a male-dominated tradition as Zen?" I asked. "It's so macho, so Japanese."

Her reply was mild, a gentle refusal to support my indignation. "In some ways I'm not in it at all. I teach and operate my little Zen center quite independently. In the ways that matter to me, these things are simply not issues—male, Japanese, and so on. They're irrelevant."

She read the disapproval on my face. "A lot of women take issue with me about this. And other things, including my name. They don't like it that I use my ex-husband's surname. Some even complain about my first name." Her glance seemed a little mischievous. "But there it is: finding out who you are, rather than trying to change it, is what this practice is all about."

She bent forward to nudge a tiny spider off the step and onto a leaf, which she carefully placed away from where people walked. I took the opportunity to study her haircut. Her hair was so short that I wondered if it was growing out from being shaved. I recalled from my stint with the Japanese Zen teacher that having one's head shaved is part of Zen ordination, after which a student is called *sensei*; a full-fledged teacher is a *roshi*.

"Are you a *roshi*?" I asked her.

"No."

"A *sensei*?"

"No."

"Are you going to be one?"

"No."

"Are you ordained as something else?"

"No."

"Well . . ."

"Well, what am I? The classic Zen question." She laughed. "I have no credentials, if that's what you're asking. In teaching, I use the term 'guide' to describe my role. For anybody who wants to follow this path, I can offer information about what I have experienced, and am experiencing, along the way. That's all. And for me this is the best way, because it avoids a lot of confusion about authority."

There was something about being with her that I liked. Was it that when I was with her I liked myself? Or maybe a better way of putting it would be to say that with her, whatever was knotty, heavy, and sticky in my personality seemed to loosen its grip on me. It was easier just to be myself. (Or maybe just to *be*, I can hear Cheri saying.) Where had I experienced that before? A memory stirred: oh, yes, with Achan, with his ease of being, which seemed to infect all those around him.

It was almost dark when Joel got back. Anna and Cheri and I helped him unload the truck, filing back and forth to the kitchen like ants, silent and single-minded: cartons of green peppers, onions, bananas, and apples; a five-gallon tub of tofu; a crate of toilet paper; a gallon each of peanut butter and sesame tahini; fifty pounds of carrots. For supper, Joel made a stir-fry with the leftovers displaced from the refrigerator by the fresh supplies. We all sat down to steaming bowls of vegetables and brown rice and macrobiotic condiments.

Anna said we needed to make a decision about where Cheri would hold guidance interviews. "We had planned to use the farmhouse, but of course now it's gone," she said. "The third floor of this building is a possibility. It's just a big open loft, though, hardly an intimate space. Or, I was thinking, we might use the sauna."

"The sauna?" Cheri inquired.

"That new little building down by the stream, behind the apple tree."

"Is it big enough? For two people on meditation cushions?"

"The platforms aren't in yet. I think it's probably just right," Anna said. "There's no door, but it's off by itself, so it's private. All it needs is some sort of step to get up into it."

"A big rock, maybe?" Cheri asked. "You've got plenty of them around here."

Joel said that in the morning he would move a rock into place. Then he asked Cheri how she had become a Zen teacher.

She said she had read D. T. Suzuki's *What Is Zen?* and taught herself to meditate from a book. Then the time came when she wanted to pursue monastic training. She sat at a monastery for a year and a half before the teacher accepted her as a monk.

Joel asked what had made her want to enter the monastery.

"We all embark on this path at the very same point," Cheri said. "And that is, when we've suffered enough."

The next morning, I typed up the daily schedule for the retreat, printed out copies, and set up a table for registration. Then I went to see if Joel needed help. He and Cheri were rolling a small boulder up to the entrance of the sauna. Cheri asked me to clear a space for it, and I brushed away rubble to make a level spot on the ground. They rolled the rock the last few inches in silence. As we were centering it in front of the sauna door, Anna walked up.

"We have a problem," Anna said. "It's been so warm that wasps have built nests over the doors into the dorm and under the porch roof around the meditation hall. I know Buddhism considers them sentient beings . . ."

A shadow of sadness crossed her face, and I thought of her cats that died in the fire.

". . . but the retreat could be ruined for some people by having to face stinging insects every time they get near a building. Not to mention having them buzz around your head during walking meditation on the porch."

"Not to cause harm," Joel said. "That's the first Buddhist precept, right?"

We all looked at Cheri. She nodded and looked at each of us, but said nothing.

Joel spoke again. "It's hard to see a nonharmful solution. Doesn't it kind of come down to wasps versus people?"

"Sentient beings against sentient beings," said Cheri, shaking her head.

She stepped up onto the rock, which wobbled treacherously, then sat down on the doorsill of the sauna. Joel twisted the rock into place until it was firmly seated.

"It's interesting to see how people come to doing no harm," Cheri said. "Often people begin by waking up to their own suffering, which sensitizes them to the suffering of others. Most of us already agree that it's not a good idea to kill people willy-nilly. But in the case of war or capital punishment or self-protection, killing people may be considered acceptable. Some people, though, begin to see that killing people in any way at all is not good. The next step is to feel that that might apply also to large animals. Animals with big brown eyes, the ones that are most like us—they're the first ones we include in not killing. But chickens? It's so hard to relate to them. Fish? Flies? Forget it. Most people have no debate at all about a mosquito. Wasps?"

The image of swatting flies and spraying wasps hung heavy in the air.

"At some point, we may begin to see it differently," Cheri went on. "One day you see a fly there in front of you, and suddenly you realize there's something going on with it, and it's the same thing that's going on with you: you're both alive. Eventually you do not harm that creature because it hurts your heart. It's just too painful to do it—not to the fly, but to you."

No one said anything. Joel and Anna seemed to be listening, as I was, with complete attention. Cheri talked on, as if considering the matter of not harming were the most important thing any of us could be doing at that moment.

"Once you awaken to the truth of our nonseparateness," she said, "you have the freedom to act boldly, with a pure heart."

I wondered what that meant.

After long moments of silence, Anna said, "Why don't we just knock down the wasps' nests around the doors? Gently. Giving them fair warning. And hope they don't rebuild before the retreat is over."

Cheri beamed. Then she bowed. I took that to mean that Anna's proposal was accepted. More than that: Anna had reached a clearer level of insight on this difficult question. I saw it not as something Anna did, but as something she received, somehow, a flash of enlightenment. The grace of that moment settled around us, and relief breathed through our little group. No killing here today.

The sun cleared the high ridge to the east, and it felt like spring. The cherry trees were beginning to bloom around the meditation hall. Anna pointed to the apple tree, covered with buds.

"In a week this place is going to look like heaven. If it stays this warm," she said to Cheri, "you could have guidance interviews outside."

Joel said that it was supposed to turn cold again. Also, he wondered if people might feel too exposed outside to talk openly about their feelings.

"Yes," said Cheri, "all that suffering. I like to call spiritual training 'the suffering to end all suffering.' People tend not to get around to this kind of practice until they've tried a lot of other things."

"How do you know whether suffering is the pain of ego—you know, not getting what you want—or the true pain of seeing separateness?" Joel asked.

"In my group in California, we've been examining this very question in regard to fear," Cheri said. "The feeling of dread can be a sign to go ahead and pursue something, just to overcome the fear that otherwise will continue to limit us. However, it's good to notice whether the dread is accompanied by 'should' messages from the ego: 'I ought to do this because . . . or 'I'll be punished if I don't . . .'—that sort of thing. Buying into those thoughts just reinforces egocentricity. What we like to call True Sickening Dread is something else: plain old fear plus the deep-down knowledge that we are going to do this thing anyway, with the willingness to go into it and see whatever we see. True Sickening Dread is a sign of courage on the spiritual path. It's not easy to tell the difference. You have to keep looking, keep trying one thing and another and noticing the consequences of what you try. Eventually, you will see what's what."

"What is it that pushes people over the hump from just reading about spiritual practice to actually meditating?" Joel asked.

"We each start on the path," Cheri repeated, "at the very same point: when we've suffered enough."

She told us how her group in California was planning to buy land for a Zen monastery and retreat center in the mountains. "We're thinking of calling it 'The Last Resort,'" she said. "Because that's what Buddhism is, for many people: the last resort."

❖ ❖ ❖

Had I suffered enough? How would I know? I longed for spiritual counsel but didn't want to ask for it. Having Jane, the Buddhist maypole of my life, torn from me had left a wound that showed no signs of healing. Along with the excitement of being in a new place and the very real pleasures I found there, I went through periods of feeling hurt, angry, confused, disconsolate. I had brought with me Jane's letter explaining why I was, basically, a hopeless case. The worst part was about what she saw as the "discontinuity" in my personality, the ways in which I would be intensely engaged and involved with something, then would abruptly drop it and take up something else. I reread the letter so often that I practically had it memorized. Each time I got to the discontinuity part, I tried to ignore the pain of admitting to myself that I had already walked away from what I had loved best in the past few years, Achan Sobin and the Buddhist Temple.

Once Cheri arrived, I began carrying Jane's letter in my pocket, hoping for an opportune moment to . . . well, to show it to her, that's really what I wanted. To say, "Look, these things have been said about me by the person who has known me most deeply. How can I know if they're true? And if they are, what can I do about it?"

One evening after Joel and I finished cleaning the kitchen and he had gone up to his room, I walked outside to sit in a lawn chair. Cheri was sitting there in the dark, drinking a cup of tea. I broached my burning subject in a vague, impersonal, roundabout way.

"In that kind of situation," Cheri said, "it can be helpful to look at oneself and ask, 'What in myself is the same as what I don't like in that other person?'"

Oh, no, it's not at all like that, I thought. I felt in my pocket for Jane's letter, my hard evidence, proving the special awfulness of my suffering. It was too dark to read. But going inside to hunt around for a flashlight would detract from the drama. Maybe I could quote those indelible phrases relating to my flawed character and paraphrase the rest. I hesitated. The right time seemed to have passed. I sensed that Cheri's response had deftly shifted the focus away from Jane and onto me—who I was, how I was.

In the same way, Cheri did not directly address the problems with meditation that I repeatedly mentioned. Instead, she pointed out an underlying habit of clinging to suffering. She could see, I think, that I did not like the phrase "clinging to suffering" and that I refused to believe I was doing that, so she mostly used other words and images. She had a seemingly endless ability to express things in fresh ways. Terms like "Buddha mind" and "big mind, small mind" also stirred my resistance, and I don't remember her ever using them, although Joel did, frequently. Eventually, after Cheri had repeatedly drawn my attention to the same pattern of thought that manifested itself in many different situations, I got the sense of what she was saying, and I had my own term for it: "something-wrong mind."

Karma was another topic about which I asked questions but got no clear answers. Cheri's responses were oblique, enigmatic, unsatisfying. If you imagine your life as a long car trip, she would say, karma is like the road map. Or was karma like the car, and dharma was the road map? All I could remember was that karma and conditioning and suffering and egocentricity were somehow equivalent. The question of what exactly karma *is* settled into a place somewhere between the questions of why Jane abandoned me and what lies ahead on a path through darkness. I just didn't know. And that, Joel said, is "don't-know mind."

CHAPTER 7

IN THE SAUNA

WHAT WE SEEK LIES IN OUR MOMENT-TO-MOMENT EXPERIENCE; WHERE TO LOOK IS ALWAYS HERE, NOW.

In the meditation hall, I arranged cushions along the sides of the room to face the walls, Zen style. Joel carefully placed a new meditation cushion and mat on the platform at the front. In the dining room, according to Cheri's instructions, we moved the tables and chairs so that everyone would face the wall during meals as well. Anna draped the library bookshelves with a sheet to help retreatants avoid the distraction of the printed word, another of Cheri's requests.

I thought about offering to put flowers on the low table at the front of the hall, but talked myself out of it. Cheri's style seemed so straightforward, so unadorned, that I thought she might find flowers fussy or churchy or, in the case of the elegant arrangement I had in mind, too imitation ikebana.

Around mid-afternoon, we heard the first car come over the ridge. The four of us stepped outdoors to watch it wind down along the far side of the cove. We were heading back inside when Cheri stopped in front of the door. Near the top of the screen, two round eyes stared out from a strangely shaped patch of fluorescent green.

"A luna moth," said Anna.

Cheri regarded it gravely. "I'm always interested in seeing who and what shows up for a retreat," she whispered.

The next few hours were filled with people and movement and chatter, a swell of activity mounted against the days of silence ahead, when the energy would be turned inward. The parking lot filled with cars, and packs and pillows and sleeping bags were carried up to the dormitory. In the dining room, people bustled around the registration table, writing checks and reading a warning about snakes and poison ivy.

Eighteen people showed up for the first retreat. All those names we had seen on registration forms, people we had corresponded with and talked to by telephone, were suddenly real beings, walking and talking all around us. Passing in and out of the kitchen as we set up the evening meal, Joel and I kept smiling at each other, as if to say, "They're here! It's happening!"

Next to the stacks of plates and bowls, Joel placed a menu board listing the dishes and noting that no meat or dairy products were used in their preparation. Next to the dishes of food was a tray of condiments—tamari, tahini, vinegar, honey, yeast, seeds, nuts, cayenne, Louisiana hot sauce, and three items I never identified, one powdered, one granulated, and one that resembled sawdust—with which, presumably, brown rice and vegetables could be amended to something more palatable. When everything was ready, Anna sounded the gong.

Some people sat down to eat with obvious relish. Others seemed taken aback at what must have been a depressing dietary prospect for the week. I saw one man return several times to the food counter, where he shook his head over a notice beside the hot water and herb tea supply: no caffeine would be served, but something called Caffix was available on request.

We all met in the meditation hall after supper to hear how the retreat would be structured. Cheri, wearing a long black skirt and black kimono top, walked to the front of the room, removed the cushion and mat from the platform, placed them on the floor, bowed, and sat down facing us. Then she outlined the schedule for sitting and walking meditation and the two work periods during the day. She asked that we follow the schedule without exception. The gong would be rung at 6:00 for wake-up and at ten minutes before each sitting. Each sitting period would last thirty minutes, beginning with the ringing of a small bell inside the hall, exactly on the stroke of the hour or half hour. No one was to enter after that bell had been rung; latecomers were obliged to meditate on the porch. We synchronized our watches to Southern Dharma time.

"What else?" Cheri asked.

"Bowing," Anna murmured. "And walking meditation."

Cheri demonstrated the Zen routine for entering and leaving the hall: bowing to the room, walking to your cushion and bowing to it, turning around and bowing to the other retreatants, taking your seat and swiveling around to face the wall, bowing when the bell was sounded to begin meditation. At the end of the meditation period, the whole procedure was reversed. She demonstrated the Zen style of walking meditation, slow half-steps with hands held at the chest. Then she described the procedure for the personal guidance interviews. You would sign up for a fifteen-minute slot, and a few minutes ahead of time you would go to the sauna. Outside would be a chair and a small gong. At the time of your appointment, you would strike the gong, and when you heard an answering bell from inside, the person ahead of you would come out, and you would go in.

Silence would be observed throughout the retreat, Cheri said. She gave no instruction in meditation, and she did not mention Buddhism.

We sat very still. The sounds outside—the stream, the wind—filled my awareness.

After a while, Cheri slid her right hand back into the kimono sleeve, where it rummaged in the deep corner and emerged with a Kleenex. I watched with rapt attention as she dabbed at her nose. Then she spoke, very softly.

"Our practice is quite simple, really. It's to pay attention. Not to do anything. Not to get anything. Not to learn anything. Not to change anything. But to pay attention, because everything you are seeking is present in each and every moment. If you're busy trying to change, you're missing it. Don't worry about trying to do life differently. Just see how it *is*."

A woman in the front of the room said that she didn't see how you could avoid trying to do things. How would you function?

Cheri stuffed the Kleenex into the opposite sleeve of her kimono. "If you are content to be with exactly what is, each moment, functioning is not a problem. You'll function as the need arises. The medieval mystic Meister Eckhart talks about having nothing, wanting nothing, needing nothing. To be completely at one with what *is* means there's nothing left over to have any difficulties. That's what this practice is about."

There was a long silence. Then Cheri spoke again.

"If I had one wish for everybody, it would be that you get really interested in how all this works. It's much more enjoyable if you remember that this is an opportunity to figure out the universe. You have this person, yourself, available for scrutiny. It's as if you put yourself under a microscope in order to find out everything there is to know about how a person operates, and then you know how *everything* operates. It's also better if you remember that this is a path of compassion, this is a process designed to end suffering. If we can find the compassion to simply sit still with *this* person," she pointed to herself, "as she or he is—not having an idea that I can improve this person or fix this person or enlighten this person, just that I'm going to sit down and be with this person—it's much easier.

"There's nowhere to go on this path. There's nothing to accomplish. The moment you move into your heart of compassion, you are there. And you don't have to be a perfect person to do that. You can simply be present to whatever you are, moment by moment by moment. You don't have to understand, you don't have to be bright or clever, you don't have to know a single thing about Buddhism. Whatever happens, embrace it in compassion, and let go of everything else."

By the next morning, it had turned cold. Sleet fell briefly, the white beads preserved in slings of spiderweb along the paths. After Joel and I removed the platform from the meditation hall, per Cheri's instruction, we carried a lawn chair and the small gong down to the apple tree by the stream. Then we put a rug in the sauna, hung an Indian blanket as a door, and installed an electric heater. A bright yellow extension cord ran conspicuously up across the road to an outlet in the barn.

"No excuse not to find the place," Cheri observed. And, indeed, the retreatants made a steady path to the chair under the apple tree, where they waited until their assigned time, then struck the gong, signaling to the pair inside the tiny building that fifteen minutes had passed.

Joel kept telling me that teachers were available to staff as well as to retreatants. If I did not seek personal guidance from teachers, he said, I would be missing an important part of what I was there for. I debated. I wanted to learn, but now I was worried about getting too involved with a particular teacher. Joel continued to urge. After several days, I admitted to myself that the main ingredient in my resistance was fear; the fierceness of Zen teachers in personal confrontations is legendary. And yet I had seen nothing in Cheri to be afraid of. Finally, I swallowed my anxieties and signed up for a turn in the sauna.

By then, it was warm and sunny. I arrived early and saw that interviews were being held outside in two lawn chairs by the stream. Waiting my turn, I wondered what I would say. I watched the monarch butterflies that had arrived with the warm weather. Hundreds of them fluttered around the flowering apple tree. Against the frothy blossoms they almost looked pasted on, like gaudy, quivering decals—a bizarre, unnerving sight. I tried to compose an intelligent question.

When my turn came, Cheri suggested that we go inside the sauna because it was getting too warm for her in the sun. We climbed in, arranged ourselves on the two black cushions, and sat. Some moments passed in silence, long, still moments, in which I noticed that, to my amazement, there was really nothing wrong.

Finally, Cheri whispered, "How can I be of assistance?"

No question came to mind. Since I did not feel free to remain silent or to say, "I don't know," I said I was confused about what I was doing in sitting meditation.

"Well," said Cheri, "let's look at it this way. That which you are seeking is that which causes you to seek. So your heart says 'Sit,' and when you sit, then you are following your heart, you are being at one with that which is guiding and directing your life."

I wondered what that meant; it sounded suspiciously theistic. She went on to say something even more surprising.

"It's not necessary to be absolutely present for extended periods in your meditation for it to have an effect. We're not measuring this in time and space. There is a way of grasping your willingness to be present that does not involve standards and competition and judging yourself and that sort of thing. It's like being in the presence of someone you really admire and respect and care a great deal for. You just don't tend to nod off, you don't daydream and make shopping lists, because you really want to be there. It's that attitude with which we can learn to sit."

"I'm a long way from that," I said. I confessed that I had begun to dread sitting, using work as an excuse to avoid it when I could.

"And how does that make you feel?" she asked.

I described the anxiety I experienced anticipating medita-tion, the frustration I felt sitting on the cushion with my mind always wandering, and the shame that sickened me when I manufactured excuses to avoid going to the meditation hall.

"Suffering. Do you see that? Do you see how it works?" Cheri asked. "You know, almost everybody I talk to about spiritual growth has one deep, underlying concern, and that is everything they're going to have to give up. It almost never occurs to anybody that all they're going to give up is suffering."

The best I could do with that idea was to stop sitting alto-gether. I knew it fell short of true acceptance, but at least it was not perpetuating the agony.

✧ ✧ ✧

Spiritual growth can take place in some pretty roundabout ways. In this instance, I suspect that temporarily giving up on meditation—or, rather, giving up stewing about it (I had yet to discover that I could stop stewing without stopping sit-ting)—helped me to stop perpetuating agonies in general. It felt so good just to be going about my life, without dragging around that pernicious sense of Something Wrong.

Now and then, I would notice that a longer time had passed—an hour or two, half a day, maybe, at that point—without any thoughts about Jane. I got curious about what pre-cipitated those thoughts, what actually happened just before all those old questions and fears and grief took me over again. Quickly I saw a pattern: when I was tired or stressed or cranky or upset, out came The Letter, literally or figuratively. It seemed as if feeling bad was a cue to make myself feel even worse. I asked Cheri if that could be true.

"Only you can answer that question," she said.

"But it makes no sense!" I exclaimed.

"No—it doesn't, does it?" she rejoined softly.

In fact, the whole mix of misery associated with losing Jane may have been the best possible preparation for meeting Cheri. I never tried to make Cheri into a mother figure, and I never imagined her to be a perfect person. As for the category I had fixed up for Spiritual Teachers (previously occupied by people who, because of ethnic origin or gender or teaching style, remained remote from me), she slipped right out of that box without my noticing. Maybe it is all a matter of personal chemistry, or maybe it is karma, but because Cheri simply seemed to be herself and allowed me to be myself, nothing stood in the way of my learning from her. And I can't help but think that for it to have worked that way, I needed to have first met Jane. Having experienced the folly of expecting someone else to be at the center of my life, I did not repeat that mistake with Cheri.

❖ ❖ ❖

A week after that first guidance appointment in the sauna, winter took a final, brief stand. A light snow fell, and the cherry boughs, which had just passed full bloom, were whitened again. Snowflakes and petals drifted together in the gray sky. The butterflies folded their wings against the sudden cold and were stilled. Along the road their carcasses littered the ground.

I wondered about suffering. As soon as I no longer expected myself to meditate twice a day, my misery over it evaporated, and my life seemed pretty wonderful; I could barely remember the feeling of unhappiness. I told Cheri if I could just continue to live in a place like Southern Dharma, I did not think I would suffer any more.

She agreed that I was probably enjoying the results of letting up on myself about meditation, and she suggested that I notice how good it felt to let go of suffering. In the long run, though, she thought it likely that I would suffer again. I was like someone who had moved from a poor neighborhood to a nice part of town, she said, and was enjoying my bright new life. But I had left behind a houseful of crying, hungry children—unacceptable aspects of myself—to whom, sooner or later, I would have to return. I was the only one who could take care of them, and it was there, and there alone, that I would learn compassion.

CHAPTER 8

WASH DISHES, RING BELLS

EGO DISCOMFORT SIGNALS SPIRITUAL OPPORTUNITY.

A few days before the next retreat, Cheri asked me how many people were signed up.

"Eleven for the whole eight days and twenty-one for the weekend," I said, looking over the registration forms. "One is a doctor just back from a Zen monastery in Japan. And there are five people from a rafting center near here. . . ."

"That might be an interesting place to visit," Cheri interjected. "I hear they teach kayaking as well as whitewater rafting."

Not that there was much time for recreation. Between retreats, we tried to catch up with maintenance and office work, and Cheri held guidance interviews. A good number of people showed up, driving the hour or two it took from civilization, meeting with her for an hour, then taking a walk or sitting outside for a while and driving back again.

When she was free, Cheri worked along with us like one of the staff. Usually she washed dishes, which she managed by pinning her kimono sleeves up to her shoulders with clothespins she kept by the sink. A routine evolved that we called Kitchen Dharma: we asked questions, and Cheri answered them, right along with whatever else we were doing.

Soon I was asking as many questions as Joel. Questions flew out of me with no hesitation, no anticipation of what the answer might be, popping out in a steady stream, like balls from a tennis machine. Cheri was in her crouch, ready to return whatever I threw her way. No matter how high or fast or far the questions were, she swung, she connected. Her racquet, of course, was the dharma. What she returned to me was more than I could deal with, but something in me was watching and listening.

I told Cheri about my image of the tennis ball machine. She said someone she spoke with regularly by telephone imagined a dharma vending machine: you put in a coin, dial Cheri's number, and out comes dharma. Someone else had compared Cheri's ongoing dharma talk to a faucet that is turned on full force and can't be turned off.

One thing I was curious about was why Cheri did not give meditation instructions at the beginning of each retreat. She said she gave them individually in guidance interviews.

"Don't you have a basic technique you want people to work with?"

"I think the technique must suit the person. You know, like the punishment fitting the crime," she laughed. "If people are already using a particular a technique, I encourage them to stick with it. If not, I generally recommend counting the breath, to begin with. And we go from there."

Joel jumped in with some complicated question about physiological reactions triggering the emotions and vice versa.

"And don't forget thought," Cheri said, "which is right in there egging it all on."

They talked for a while about things I had never heard of, the kinds of things you learned only with a lot of sitting experience, I figured.

When there was a gap in the discussion, I turned to Cheri. I was beginning to see, I said, that meditation was the only really important thing to pursue.

"Good!" she replied. "There's an old Zen saying: Practice as if your hair is on fire. That means, don't wait. We have this tendency to put other things first."

Was that a comment on my not showing up for the daily sittings? If so, it was a gentle one. I was moved to confess to Cheri that I had expected to be intimidated by a Zen teacher, to be pushed to my limits, or even beyond, and I was relieved that she was so easy to be with.

"Ah, the teacher's job is precisely to push you beyond your limits," she said. "But you have to be near a limit for the teacher to have something to push against."

I asked how you knew if you were near a limit.

She smiled. "There's an unmistakable discomfort, which is your ego feeling threatened. We call that a spiritual opportunity. It's gotten to be a joke at our center; anything awful is called an 'opportunity.' Everybody laughs about it, but in fact it's a major step in your practice when you get the sense of that—that your resistance to something is your chance to understand how you work, how you suffer. Your resistance becomes a signal to look carefully at what's going on."

Anna wondered if it was unrealistic to expect that many people would ever meditate regularly; people are just too busy.

Cheri agreed. "'The still, small voice is well and good,' we say, 'but I have important things to do.'"

"That's what I mean," Anna said.

"But how do we decide what's important?" Cheri asked. "It's good to look at that process. Every moment we make a choice. 'What's important now?'"

Anna persisted. "Maybe we decide that other things are more important, like responsibilities to other people, and we really don't have time for meditation."

"There's plenty of time for everything," Cheri asserted gently, "once we give up having our own way."

Now, there was something I simply could not fathom. Who would want to give up having their own way? Why would they want to?

Cheri recommended that we read something relevant by Meister Eckhart, then went on. "Once we realize that our experience of everything is within ourselves, then we're turning to the one place where something can be done about suffering. If it's happening out there, external to us, there's no hope. We'd have to fix the entire world. But if the suffering is all in here, if it's *this* that's creating it," she pointed to herself, "well, maybe there's some cleaning up that can be done."

"Yeah," Joel sighed. "We're all in the same boat on the sea of suffering, and the answer is the same for everybody: work on yourself. Right?"

Cheri agreed, explaining that the work involves being willing to see everything there is to see. "If you want to be right, to be noble and good and smart and charming and all those things, you cannot afford to look honestly at yourself. You will have to look very, very selectively. And you have to project an awful lot of your own experience out there onto the world and deny that it has anything to do with you."

"Wait a minute," I interjected, "you're saying there's something wrong with being good?"

To *want* to be good is no better or worse than wanting to be bad, she said. Both arise from egocentricity, both support the sense of separateness, which is the root of suffering.

I was agitated, full of argument, but couldn't find words for my feelings.

"Instead of wanting to be this way or that way, if what you want is to know *what is so*," Cheri said, "then it's simple. Just adopt the willingness to take absolute responsibility for every single thing you experience. There is no blame in it, no guilt. It's just acknowledging that this is me, this is mine, my situation, my life, my perceptions. What am I doing? Instead of trying to figure out what everybody else is doing and why they're doing it and what's going on with them and how to make it work for you—all that just maintains egocentricity—stop and say, 'It's all mine, but no blame. And I take absolute responsibility for every single second of my life.'" She looked at me. "Get it?"

"Not really, no."

"If everything is yours, everything is you, it's no longer in your interest to cause harm. But let's keep this simple, let's make it entirely practical. I invite you to try this. Accept full responsibility for everything in your life. Then practice as if your hair is on fire."

❖   ❖   ❖

The first night of the retreat, Joel and Anna and I rushed through the kitchen cleanup so we would be free in time for Cheri's introductory talk. It was actually a setting forth of the many guidelines for functioning in silence, but Cheri never missed an opportunity for dispensing dharma, and we didn't want to miss a word. Even more than that, for me it was wonderfully exhilarating and also somehow poignant to be present at that gathering of souls who were embarking on a journey into themselves.

I remember taking my seat in the back corner of the meditation hall, facing the wall, and waiting in a state of superalertness. At the beginning of a retreat, even a minute with nothing happening can seem interminable, and the pause before the teacher speaks is energized with anticipation. For many of us, whatever our commitment to sitting meditation may be, at some level, this is what we have come for: the answers, from the authority. But maybe the introductory pause is a subtle pedagogical technique for demonstrating what the process is all about, a way of prolonging heightened attention within the perfect stillness and quiet of that spacious moment before the first word. When else are you that awake?

"Please turn and face this way."

Hardly more than a whisper, Cheri's voice filled the room.

"What would you like to talk about?"

A long, still silence.

"Well, how about sitting practice?" she said. "Since that's what we're here for."

Silence, ringing with anticipation.

"We tend to think, 'Sitting is all well and good, but I have something important to do. I just don't have time.' But the real trick of it is finding the willingness. When we're willing, everything is easy. There's plenty of time, plenty of opportunity, we have enough energy. A large part of finding that willingness is letting go of the notions we have about fitting our spiritual practice into a certain framework. We can't fit spiritual training into our lives: we must fit our lives into spiritual training. When it begins to dawn on us that there is no life apart from spiritual training, then we begin to practice."

She explained the schedule for sitting and the procedure for guidance interviews, and she answered a few questions. When she finished, we were still sitting, just sitting together through another very long pause, alert, but free now of the tension of anticipation.

"Thank you," Cheri whispered, bowing. "The silence begins now."

We left the hall in a file, each person stopping and turning to bow before passing through the door. The planks of the porch gave little creaks, then footsteps slapped lightly on the pathway back to the main building. Through the clear air, you could hear the rush and burble of the stream down the hill. The sky was still deep blue between the dark silhouetted trees toward the west, but overhead it was already inky black, all the stars right there. People stopped in the path, looking up, silent.

✧ ✧ ✧

The next day began with a fiasco.

While Cheri conducted guidance interviews, someone else was needed to ring the bell in the meditation hall to signal the beginning and end of each sitting and walking period. Cheri asked Anna to do it. But Anna had to deal with a plumbing problem, and she forgot to go to the meditation hall. No bells were rung. As a result, the retreatants sat continuously for several hours with no intervals for walking, a feat of endurance not usually asked even of advanced students. Finally, someone got up and found Joel, who calmly rang the bell to end the sitting period and declared free time until lunch.

Anna felt terrible. Cheri, though, was amused. She remarked that nothing so out of the ordinary had happened in her entire time at the monastery.

That night, Joel and I were in the kitchen drinking tea and talking softly about how to organize things better for the following day. As I fished my tea bag from the cup and dropped it into the compost bucket, Cheri came through the door. She moved beside me, leaned onto the counter, and said quietly, "Would you lead the meditation tomorrow?"

"What?" I said.

"Would you lead the meditation tomorrow?"

"You mean—?"

"Sit in the meditation hall and be in charge."

"You mean sit in front and keep time?"

"Yes. Ring the bells and lead the walking."

"Me?" I heard myself say it: "Why me?"

"I will be having guidance interviews. Joel will be cooking. Anna has to go into town."

"I can't. I've got too much else to do."

Joel said good night and left. Cheri said nothing, and nothing showed on her face. She just stood there.

"Look, I really cannot do it," I said defensively. "I've been helping in the kitchen every day and putting off other things that have to be done. Tomorrow I've got to work on the mailing list."

She turned without saying a word and disappeared silently through the swinging door. I took my tea out to the library where I lifted a corner of the sheet covering the bookshelves. I glanced at the Zen books but chose instead a book of Meister Eckhart's writings and took it upstairs with me. I thought no more about the kitchen discussion until I had gotten ready for bed and gone down the hall to the bathroom.

At some point, I became aware of having been in the bathroom for an indeterminate period. I was intensely absorbed in conversation with myself—for a much longer time, it struck me, than I ever managed to keep my mind on anything in meditation. The conversation consisted of my arguments for not leading meditation the next day, interpolated with snatches of things I remembered Cheri saying.

"I have an obligation," I said to myself, "to do my job, to finish what I've started."

Have you noticed the tendency to put everything else before spiritual practice?

"But I am not here for practice. I am here to work."

The still, small voice is well and good, we say, but I have more important things to do.

"I'd do it another time, gladly, but not tomorrow, because if I don't get that mailing out Saturday morning, we lose a whole day!"

There's plenty of time for everything once we give up having our own way.

"No, it really isn't that. I just want . . ."

Suddenly, hearing my own words, I saw how I was doing exactly what Cheri had described. She had said, "People do not want to put spiritual practice first." I had replied, "It is more important than anything, I am going to make a real commitment." She had said, "People say that, but at the first opportunity they seem to find other things to do." I faced the simple truth: I did not want to spend a whole day in meditation. I felt exasperated, as if she had won an undeclared contest.

For quite a while, I sat there in the bathroom, overcome with chagrin. Then, for an instant, I considered that I could undo my decision. But the resistance reasserted itself: no, no, no, I really did have all those things I wanted to get done, I truly needed to get done, and I had counted on doing them tomorrow.

Every moment you make a choice. What's important now? And now? And now?

All my objections were countered with things she had said.

My final argument was desperate. "But I've been helping all week in the kitchen and even with Anna's projects, and I don't have time for my own work! I'm tired of this! I've been patient so far, but I have my limits!"

Limits: the magic word. If a dove had descended bearing a card on which was lettered OPPORTUNITY, the message could not have been clearer. I had reached a limit, albeit a seemingly petty one, and the teacher was pushing me against it. I returned to my room, found a scrap of paper and wrote on it, in grudging acquiescence, *OK, I'll do it,* and scrawled my name. I tiptoed down the hall and slid it under the edge of Cheri's door.

Then I went back, got in bed, and opened the book on Meister Eckhart. The first piece was on obedience. Within the stiff, remote, old-fashioned language, something fresh and yet familiar struck me. Meister Eckhart made clear the purpose of obedience in spiritual training: it weakens the grip of ego. It is not personal. It is not punishment. It is a practical means to a spiritual end.

I felt shaken, and grateful. This opportunity had not simply happened, it had been handed to me as a gift. I got out of bed, took a pencil and the book to write on, and padded down the hall again. I retrieved my note and wrote at the bottom *Thank you*, and slid it back under the door.

I was awake much of the night, anxious about the day ahead. At best, it would be grueling. At worst . . . I braced myself against the possibility that I would be unequal to the task. In the morning, before I had a chance to find out if Cheri had read my note or to say anything to her about my change of heart or my anxieties, I met her on the stairs. Without a word or a look, she handed me a sheet of typed instructions for keeping time and leading the walking meditation.

Nothing about the day was as I had anticipated. Instead of the minutes and hours feeling long and tedious, time, for the most part, was not an issue. The day stretched so long ahead of me that it seemed infinite, and I simply gave myself up to it. Instead of feeling self-conscious, I discovered that, with the retreatants facing the walls, the seat at the front of the room is the only one from which you can see everyone and not be seen yourself. In my usual place in the back corner near the door, I had often wondered if my fidgeting could be observed, and the answer clearly was yes. But now that I was invisible to the others, instead of the usual strain I felt in meditation, sitting was effortless, and I sat very still. Covert reviews of the instruction sheet, which I slid under the edge of the meditation mat, were easily accomplished. Even ringing the little brass bell required no special skill, just attention. When I struck the bell to end the first sitting, it was with confidence that the task at hand was manageable after all. I bowed and rose, carefully holding the bell, waited until everyone was standing, then bowed again, turned, and began to lead the walking meditation.

Slow, formal, Zen half-steps, placing the right foot, then pausing, shifting the weight, placing the left foot slightly ahead, pausing. Bell, on its little cushion, balanced in one hand, striker in the other. All it takes is attention. Bowing while holding the bell was going to be another challenge, but I knew I could do it. Leading meditation was just another job that had to be done, like washing dishes. Somebody had to ring the bells for sitting and walking, and today it was my turn.

In perfectly measured movement, we inched silently around the room. After twenty-five minutes, as prescribed on the instruction sheet, I struck the bell to signal five minutes of "fast walking," meaning a brisk normal pace, before the next half hour of sitting.

No one seemed to recognize the signal. Instead of walking fast, they began to return at the same slow pace to their cushions. To my consternation, some even sat down. I considered doing the same; I could have pretended to misunderstand the instructions. It was all so terribly embarrassing. I struggled with my options, finally emitting an audible sigh—further embarrassment—as I accepted that I was there not to save face, but to practice obedience.

I walked fast. Those who were still on their feet glanced furtively around and took the cue. Some of those who had resumed sitting stood up again, and, with expressions of panicked sheep, joined the fast-walkers. The others maintained their dignity by sitting very still.

I fumed as I walked. The retreatants and I obviously had received different instructions. How could Cheri do this to me?

When the five minutes were up, I struck the bell and with relief returned to my cushion. Again we sat.

After the second sitting, I rang the bell for walking and stood up. Everyone rose and turned and walked. The person who had been next to my usual spot in the back corner took a few steps, reached the door, turned, bowed, and exited. No problem: he either had a guidance interview or needed to go to the bathroom. After another few steps, the next person also bowed and left. As if some invisible wall deflected them from the well-worn orbit around the room and redirected them out the door, each person bowed, and, one by one, stepped out of the hall.

I was left alone, in acute distress. I figured that four of them had fifteen-minute guidance interviews during the hour, and maybe four more were leaving for bathroom breaks. But the rest? Following the whims of their egos! I watched my self-righteousness rise up, then tried to let it go.

Solitary circumambulation felt ridiculous, but I walked alone for twenty minutes. Then one person came in and walked with me, until I rang the bell for fast-walking, when he sat down. As other retreatants returned to the room and took their seats, again I fast-walked alone. It is not an easy thing to do, from the perspective of ego.

I spent the next sitting period worrying about how to handle the next fast-walk. I had not arrived at a solution when the third walking period began.

What would be the Zen approach to such a problem? I asked myself.

And the answer came: do the obvious.

After twenty-five minutes of walking, I stopped, struck the bell, and announced, "Fast-walking."

Everybody fast-walked. I was stunned; I was joyous. A triumph of Zen directness and simplicity!

During the morning work period, I completed the mailing list, and during the rest period, I took it to the mailbox. On the way back, I lay down among wild strawberry blossoms in a little meadow and looked at the sky. I had accomplished everything I wanted to do, plus doing nothing. Somehow, submitting to a schedule had opened up time; discipline had created freedom. Mindlessly working nonstop, I realized, is not discipline. The awareness that week after week had passed without my once finding time to walk up to the top of the mountain filled me with regret.

The last walking meditation of the afternoon was from 4:30 to 5:00. Feeling, in my expansiveness, that I could handle anything, I led the group outside onto the porch. In soft, slow, measured treads, we circled the building. The north and east sides were in shade, the west and south brightly lit by the afternoon sun. As I turned a corner, for several seconds one bare foot rested on boards that were distinctly cool, the other on sun-warmed wood. Then the next step: both feet on warm wood. A few wasps buzzed overhead. A bird fluttered out of a nest under the eaves. An occasional creak from a board.

Toward the end of the walking, I realized I had no idea what to do at 5:00, when Cheri normally appeared. Would she show up to lead the final sitting? Should I vacate the spot at the front so she could take it or stay there until she arrived and then get up?

Surely the Zen way was to wait and see. Meanwhile, as we inched along the last few yards toward the door, I scanned the path to the main building as well as I could without turning my head. No sign of Cheri. My anxiety mounted as we filed back into the hall. Anticipating an awkward, unseemly, terribly un-Zenlike blundering through a changing of the guard, I returned to the cushion in the front of the room. I waited a few seconds past 5:00, giving her plenty of time, before striking the bell.

At least it was over for another half hour. There was nothing to do but sit. My dread lifted. I settled down to meditate, glancing around the room one last time. Then I noticed a black-robed form on the cushion in the far back corner. There, on "my" cushion, sat the teacher. And here I sat, on "hers." But the universe seemed not to notice this breach of protocol; the silence was undisturbed. A cushion is just a cushion, the space in the meditation hall is the same in the front as in the back, and here we sit.

CHAPTER 9

WHO ARE THE SENTIENT BEINGS
WE VOW TO SAVE?

HOW LITTLE WE KNOW OF OURSELVES UNTIL WE BEGIN
TO LOOK WITHIN.

After leading meditation for a whole day, my attitude toward sitting completely turned around, and, for a while, anyway, I became eager to put in time on the cushion. Joel suggested not only that I sign up for guidance interviews during the next retreat but also that I join the retreatants for the first and last sittings each day.

Once the weather warmed up, Joel stopped going to the meditation hall before the wake-up bell to build a fire in the woodstove. No matter that the mountain air was still cold at night, and the hall held the chill through the day. Most of the retreatants were, like Joel, outdoor types, with hardy anatomies and insulated outfits, and for them cold was not a problem. But I was not one of them. Halfway through the morning sitting, I feared, I would be cold to the bone.

I arrived at the hall the first morning wearing heavy tights under a wool skirt, two pairs of socks, several sweaters, and a wool shawl. Then, through the door, I saw a heartening sight: Cheri herself stoking the woodstove. The room radiated an un-Zen-like toastiness. I stepped out of my shoes, painfully tight over the thick socks, took off two of the sweaters, and as I entered, made a deeper bow than usual.

Feeling a special closeness to Cheri, born of the idea that she had made the fire *for me*, I decided to ask her about putting some apple blossoms on the table at the front of the hall. During the rest period after lunch, I was writing her a note when she came up and motioned for me to follow her outside. Her whisper had an edge to it, as she reminded me that the procedure is to take off shoes before entering the meditation hall and put them on again before walking outside. I was the only one, she had observed, who did walking meditation on the porch either barefoot or in socks, which meant I was tracking dirt into the hall.

A tempest of self-defense and sarcastic counterattack boiled up in my mind. "Isn't that a little extreme?" I wanted to say. But I just bowed, a small bow this time. As I walked back through the dining room, more or less crushed, I wadded up my note about the flowers and threw it away.

When I sat down in the sauna for my guidance interview, Cheri was as cheerful as ever, as if the issue of the shoes had never come up. That threw me—I was prepared to defend myself or to acknowledge guilt (I hadn't decided which), but it was clear that Cheri had left that issue behind. For a moment, I cast around for something to say, then described how difficult it was to keep my attention on my breath, how I could not manage to watch thoughts, feelings, and daydreams without getting lost in them.

"Let me tell you," Cheri said, "about an image I find useful." She described a doll made by Indians in the Southwest, a big doll onto which are fastened many little dolls that can be removed. She called it a storytelling doll. "The little dolls run around and act out stories, and the big doll functions as home base. All the drama takes place in front of the big doll, who just sits there, observing without getting involved. You are the big doll. Your job is simply to watch."

I could see it in my mind: sitting on my cushion as the big doll, immovable as a Buddha, patient as a mother, watching the agitations of my mind as played out by various aspects of myself.

When you hear within yourself one of those all-too-familiar voices, Cheri said, saying things you've said to yourself a thousand times, just take a look at whatever drama is being acted out and see who's talking. You'll discover that most of your life is being run by subpersonalities you aren't even aware of.

I thought of the voices I had come to notice in meditation. Mostly, they were planning ahead. *When I get out of here, I'm going back to the office and . . . then tomorrow I'll . . . and next week . . .*

"Mainly I hear a planner," I said, disappointed that it was something so mundane.

She told me to take a good look at the planner. What could I learn about that part of myself? I might, for example, observe that the planner has a worried look. I might discover some tension or an area of tightness in my body that I had not noticed before. She assured me that I would have many opportunities to see the planner, as well as lots of other subpersonalities.

"When one of them begins to take over with some drama or another, acknowledge its needs, with total understanding and acceptance and compassion. But then ask it to settle down. Offer it, perhaps, its own little meditation cushion," Cheri smiled, "and turn your attention back to the breath. The big doll just keeps sitting. Lots of stories will get told by all these little dolls, and if you keep watching you'll see them all."

I nodded.

"Have you ever watched a cat watching something?" she asked. "Your job is to watch in that same way, like the proverbial cat at a mouse hole. The cat will sit there absolutely unmoving, totally absorbed and alert, and very, very patient. The cat doesn't go to sleep or wander off. Nor does it get bored and make a dive at the hole, demanding that the mouse come out. No, no. It sits still and keeps watching. This is how we practice: pay attention, keep looking. You know there's something there you want, and you make yourself absolutely available. It doesn't do to be too eager or too distant. You just watch as if your life depended on it. Which, in fact, it does."

Those little people within you, she said, that troublesome population of subpersonalities, make up egocentricity. Those are conditioned aspects of you. When you have watched them so long and with such acceptance that they no longer rule your life, then you may find the willingness to let them all go. You will know all there is to know about yourself, and you will see that you have known it all along. "Since before the beginning of beginningless time," she said. "Then you can give up having your own way about things. Which, of course, we so rarely do, which is why we suffer. We cease to suffer once we can say, 'Have it your way.' Or 'Thy will, not mine, be done.'"

Whose way? I wondered. Whose will?

"Remember Meister Eckhart," Cheri went on. "If you are absolutely content to be with exactly what is, as is, each moment, you don't have any problems."

My time was up. I thanked her for the warmth of the meditation hall and remarked that my image of Zen was that it was too macho for things like creature comforts, not to mention storytelling dolls.

"I see no reason to add discomfort to what we already suffer," Cheri said, "nor to avoid anything that is useful in helping us to wake up."

✧　✧　✧

People from the rafting center had showed up for each of the retreats, evidently attracted by the down-to-earth nature of the practice. One of them, Raul, told Cheri that he was relieved that there was no incense or chanting or foreign words or rituals and no philosophical stuff. Cheri herself called it the "no-frills path," asserting that Zen is purely practical.

"There's nothing mysterious about it," she liked to say, "if you discount, of course, the utter mysteriousness of everything."

When Raul invited Cheri to lead a half-day workshop at the rafting center, she asked me to come along. My initial reaction was to decline. For one thing, those hardy souls—and Cheri was one of them—might want to follow up the workshop with whitewater rafting or a bike ride (in the mountains!) or some similarly terrifying activity. Also, my current aim in life was to store up the benefits of solitude and silence, and spending time away from the retreat center was not in my plan. All that resistance was overcome, however, by my curiosity about how Cheri would be in what I thought of as "real life," and at the last minute I decided to go.

The workshop was called "Projection." That sounded more psychological than spiritual, I noted, but Cheri assured me that for our purposes, they were the same and that a psychological slant would work better for the rafting center. She began the workshop by leading us in exercises to demonstrate how we project our own concerns onto the world, how we attribute our own experience to others. A handful of people seemed to get it right away; they nodded and smiled. Others, no doubt, were skeptical, and I suspected most were simply baffled. One woman was immediately resistant.

"I don't get it. A quality I notice in this other person is that he is tall. But I am short, so how can that be my projection?"

"Short and tall are two sides of one issue, and it's the issue that's yours," Cheri said. "The tall person may not have thought once about your being short, unless that's an issue for him too."

I found it contrary to common sense that everything we see is our own projection. On the other hand, I could not help wondering why a Zen teacher would present this issue so persuasively if it were not true, and important.

"The point of this," Cheri was saying, "is to realize that all you can do is take full responsibility for yourself—and for the whole world. All that matters is how *you* live each moment, learning to listen to your heart as your guide."

Raul asked what she meant by heart.

"Awareness, intuition. The still, small voice. We might even call it the voice of truth. Every moment it's there, guiding you. Do you have this experience?"

Some people nodded. "Sometimes," one said.

"But it's always there." Cheri leaned forward and seemed to be looking at all of us at once, eager for us to understand. "It seems as if it's there only sometimes, and the rest of the time it's not available. But no, *we* are not available; *it* is always there. There aren't many absolutes in this, but here is one of them: the still, small voice of our heart is always available."

"How do you find it?" someone asked.

Cheri beamed. "It looks as if there's no way to avoid the subject of meditation, is there? Meditation is the traditional way of discovering this voice and learning to listen to it."

Around the room, people shifted positions in their chairs.

"Our tendency is to respond to a recommendation that we take up meditation by thinking we have more important things to do," Cheri said. "'I've got a deadline,' we say. 'I don't have time for this intuition business.' And so we go about working toward our deadline; then something else important comes up. What to do? Both things feel important. Now, if we haven't let go of our habitual sense of guilt and fear and deprivation, we're going to be worried. Are we doing the right thing? What's going to happen? Will we make a mistake? On and on and on. The fact is, the deadline will come, and we will meet it or we won't. It's as simple as that. But we want a guarantee. We don't want to do something unless we know it's going to pay off in the way we expect."

A chorus of agreement.

"But that takes all the *fun* out of life!" Cheri's voice suddenly reverberated through the room. "There *aren't* any guarantees. The only guarantee is that if you operate from fear, you're always going to feel deprived, no matter how much you have."

"Why?" One voice spoke for many of us.

"Because it's all an attitude of mind. It has nothing to do with the circumstances."

"I don't know what you mean by that," someone else said.

"We have no control over what we get," Cheri explained. "We have absolute control over what we do. We don't have to suffer. It's not a requirement. No matter what happens." A pause, then her near-whisper. "Can you see how that takes the pressure out of making choices?"

Some saw, presumably. Some did not. Some, like me, weren't sure but stumbled between a feeling of having gotten it and wondering what exactly it was that we'd gotten.

When I turned my attention back to Cheri, she was talking about child abuse, saying that we project our own qualities onto the abuser.

"When you look at another person and think of the cruelty or malice or hatefulness of their actions, those feelings are in yourself. It is impossible to know a quality in that other person unless you know it in yourself."

Chairs squeaked, feet shuffled. Arms tightened across chests.

"Here's a child molester, let's say, very likely someone who has been mistreated all of his or her life. Let's just say 'his.' He was abused as a child, emotionally or physically. Nobody loved him, nobody took care of him, nobody talked with him or listened to him. Now he finds himself driven to molesting children. He hates himself, he knows society hates him, but he cannot stop."

Silence.

"We may say this person is despicable, even that he should be killed. We pass judgment. Then we walk away, while in our own lives we cannot—what? What is it for you? Can't not eat chocolate? Can't stay away from sugar? Can't stop being sexual? Can't control anger?"

Two people got up and walked out without saying anything. Alarm rang through me.

Cheri continued in a soft voice. "I'm truly glad that for me it's sugar and not little children. Because I cannot sit here and be smug enough to say I know I would find the strength of character to overcome that."

I was appalled by this triple lapse: that she would include herself in the same category as a child molester, that she would admit to uncontrollable craving, and—even worse, in a way— that the craving be for something so trivial as sugar. All those diet colas . . .

"The work to be done is here, with me," I heard her saying, as if from a great distance, "and if I can't perfect myself, I cannot worry about someone else's imperfections. If I see their imperfection, then I must have that same imperfection within myself."

The room was closing in on me. Cheri's voice seemed farther and farther away.

"That's projection," she went on. "As one of my favorite spiritual teachers, Rajneesh, liked to say . . ."

No, no, no, something in me screamed. My mind raced chaotically as I tried to figure out what was wrong, then the floor rose beneath me, and I knew I was about to faint or be sick or go crazy. I judged the easiest path to the door, edged off my chair, and crept outside.

Huddled on the walkway, I closed my eyes and held tight. Everything was obliterated by my physical distress. I sat paralyzed, as if on the edge of a precipice, where the slightest motion would dislodge me and I would fall to my death (or, more likely, throw up, which is the same as death, from an ego point of view). After what seemed like an awfully long time, my body relaxed a little, and my breathing settled.

Through the open door, I heard Cheri conclude the workshop with an assignment.

"Do you all know what a koan is?" she asked. "It's a riddle, used as a teaching tool in a particular Zen tradition. The teacher poses the koan, and the student tries to answer it. The purpose of the koan is to jolt the mind out of its usual ruts. Now, I don't belong to the tradition that uses koans, so we won't get into this in a formal way. But just in case it's helpful, I want to pose this little puzzle. One of the vows that is recited each day in Zen monasteries is 'to save all sentient beings.' It's called the bodhisattva vow. Bodhisattvas are beings who postpone their own final enlightenment in order to save everyone who is still suffering. Now here's the question: what does it mean to save all sentient beings?"

Silence. Then she must have bowed to signal that it was time for a break, because people began coming out. I got to my feet, trying to look casual. Cheri asked me what had happened, why I had left. I felt under some momentary stress, I said, which had something to do with what she had been saying.

"I can pretty much guarantee that it has everything to do with *you*. Projection—remember?" she said blithely. "Although I'm the first to admit that I am not one of your tea-sipping, cherry-blossom-contemplating Zen teachers. In case that's what's bothering you. Not my style."

I turned away from her gaze.

Her style may have deterred some people, but the second part of the workshop was full. No mention was made of the vow to save all sentient beings.

After lunch, Raul told Cheri that the rafting center was inviting her to return in the fall for a week of workshops that would include meditation. So many people wanted to see her individually that Cheri agreed to stay the rest of that day and give guidance interviews. She asked me to meet her in the restaurant at 7:00.

Projection, I decided, was something I wanted to look into on my own before pursuing it further with Cheri. I spent the afternoon walking and sitting by the river and pondering. Then I waited in the restaurant, drinking tea and watching the scene below. Canoes zipped and glided through the rushing water, and rafts full of people bounced down the river in explosions of yellow life jackets and whitewater and shrieks of excitement. A kayaker practiced the last stretch of rapids, paddling upstream, turning and shooting smoothly down between the rocks, then rolling over in the deep pool at the bottom and rolling up again.

I was finishing a bowl of soup when Cheri arrived, right on time. She ordered a diet cola and an elaborate dessert that Raul had told her was the best thing on the menu. I made up my mind not to point out the obvious contradiction. But I did mention the potentially harmful effects of drinking too much diet cola.

Ignoring my comments, Cheri asked what I had thought of the workshop. I said I was impressed that so many energetic outdoorsy types were drawn to an introspective pursuit. On the other hand, maybe it was easy for them to be fearless and attentive, because they operated in an environment that so thoroughly reinforced, even demanded, those qualities.

"You did notice, I hope, that they have their own limits," Cheri pointed out. "That they withdraw and push away whatever is scary for them. As we all do, of course, each with our own issues."

She went on talking, about how sitting meditation is analogous to paddling, how much easier it is to go with the current than against it, how to accept the flow and, with much practice, learn to maneuver within it; how you stay with it, one moment at a time, facing whatever comes up, simply doing the best you can.

"Well, that's what I'm saying," I rejoined. "When you're paddling through rapids, it's not so hard to stay with it, because the consequences of letting your attention wander are so serious."

"And the consequences of not paying attention to your life?" Cheri asked.

I could not think of any reply.

She talked then about fear. If you don't know what you are afraid of, she said, or even that you are afraid, you're probably living a restricted life, avoiding things you might enjoy, putting energy into *not* doing things, whether you are aware of it or not.

Fear wasn't a problem for me, I said. Cheri looked me in the eye and said nothing.

A fly circled the dish in front of her and landed in the mountain of dark chocolate. Cheri extricated it with a corner of her napkin, raised the window next to our table, and deposited the fly on the sill, where it licked its legs and flew away.

❖   ❖   ❖

I have at times suspected Cheri of plotting elaborate schemes to demonstrate to me how trapped I am in my conditioning, how limited I am by ideas of myself that I take as truth. My suspicion arises not because she appears at all calculating but because of repeated, inexplicable collusions of circumstance that unfold so perfectly to teach me what I need to know. When I have asked Cheri if she plays a role in stage-managing these spiritual dramas, she always denies it.

"I know what you mean, though," she says. "I used to be convinced that my teacher stayed up nights devising ways to torture my ego."

What to make of this, how it works, I have no idea. I have simply learned to submit to the process. Over time, I have gained a certain faith that I will come out of spiritually difficult situations into greater safety and ease and clarity—and, yes, love—than I could have imagined. A case in point was how Cheri took me by the hand, so to speak, and led me to encounter fear I didn't even know I had.

CHAPTER 10

FEAR

**NONSEPARATENESS IN ONE EASY STEP: FIND COMPASSION
FOR YOURSELF, AND YOU WILL AUTOMATICALLY HAVE IT
FOR OTHERS.**

Back at Southern Dharma the next day, while Cheri saw a few people who had come for individual appointments, Joel and I cleaned the meditation hall. I asked him about projection. He did not respond right away, and we cleared the floor in silence, gathering two or three cushions at a time and stacking them at the back of the room. When all the cushions had been moved, Joel said he had a sense of what Cheri was talking about, but he thought of it in different terms. The point is that if you keep noticing how you create your own reality—how what you call "reality" actually arises from you—you eventually realize the oneness of it all, or nonseparateness, as Cheri called it.

"Do you understand nonseparateness?" I asked.

"No," he said simply.

To me, the vow "to save all sentient beings" sounded incompatible with the idea of nonseparateness. I said so to Joel. He just shrugged and smiled at the empty room.

I pushed the wide broom slowly from one end of the hall to the other, trying to maintain mindfulness, while Joel cleaned the woodstove and brought in firewood.

"Here's a story I like," Joel said. "A Buddhist monk was living in a hut owned by an old lady. The old lady sent a young woman down to tempt him, but the monk wouldn't have anything to do with her. The old lady was furious and burned his hut down."

"I don't get it. And I certainly don't see what it has to do with projection," I said.

Joel shrugged again. "I guess that's something you find out when you experience nonseparateness."

Are we caught in circular reasoning here, or what? I thought to myself. But it was no good pressing such points with Joel or, for that matter, with Cheri. Let it go, I thought. Just drop it. When in doubt, just breathe.

As we left the meditation hall, through the trees we saw a flame-red car parked below us. It was big and boatlike, battered and rusty. The Southern Dharma parking lot, accustomed to Japanese cars, small trucks, vans, and the occasional Jeep, had probably never held such a car. It was like a pair of scruffy black and white wingtips among Birkenstocks and running shoes. We had not been expecting anyone, and we were not used to strangers showing up unannounced. Joel and I walked to the main building, saying nothing, but sharing a sense of foreboding.

In the kitchen, Anna was standing with a man who matched the car: huge, hulking, red haired, red faced, rough and worn and tense, incongruous in the gentle atmosphere of the retreat center. Anna introduced him as Roy and told us he was looking for a place to stay in exchange for work. Roy scarcely looked at us and said nothing.

Anna had told Roy he could sleep in the room that had been fixed up in the loft over the barn. The plan was that he would help her build drawers for the storage spaces under the beds in the dormitory rooms. After Roy went down to the barn, Joel and I told Anna we were not comfortable with her decision. She was concerned that we were concerned, but assured us that it would all work out. Since Roy had said he wanted to fast and to keep silent, she thought we probably would not see much of him.

"Anna, I appreciate your compassion for this guy," Joel said, "but I just don't think it's a good idea to have drifters at Southern Dharma."

"He's not a drifter," Anna said. "He works on shrimp boats in the Gulf, and it's between seasons now, or something. And you know this place is open to anybody. And he's a meditator. He found out about us from a sitting group in New Orleans."

The next morning, Roy arrived at the dormitory with the first drawer, which he had built from Anna's prototype. Joel and I had agreed to put our prejudice aside and to focus on the contribution Roy was making to the retreat center. We followed him into the first dorm room. He slid the drawer onto the tracks and pushed it closed, flush with the outside.

"Oh—it needs a lip around the edge so it won't push through," Joel said.

Roy jerked the drawer out and flung himself around to face us. His eyes flashed blue fire.

"This is how she told me to make it!" he said furiously.

"But—" Joel began.

"Don't tell me what to do!" Roy exploded. "I said I wasn't going to talk to anybody!"

He gripped the drawer menacingly, and I was afraid he might strike Joel with it.

"Okay," Joel said, "I'm sorry."

Roy stomped out of the building.

When we told the others what had happened, Cheri suggested that fasting might not be a good idea for someone who was already so volatile. But, being partial to the carpentry project, she thought we should let Roy stay if he agreed to take meals, to talk with us, to refrain from angry outbursts, and to join us for sitting meditation twice a day.

Anna conveyed Cheri's proposal to Roy, and he accepted the conditions, as long as he did not have to bring the completed drawers up to the dormitory. I still thought it was a terrible idea and said so to Cheri. I was acutely uncomfortable with Roy around.

"Maybe you could try doing the opposite of what you feel," she suggested. "Do something nice for him, something to make you feel closer to him rather than creating more distance."

"But I don't want to be close to him!" I protested.

"Have you noticed any feeling of kindness toward him? Or maybe just tolerance? Do we have anything to work with along those lines?"

"No. My feeling toward Roy is fear, pure and simple."

Cheri assured me that fear is a wonderful spiritual opportunity, which she hoped we would explore together. At the moment, though, she needed to call her Zen center in California. Southern Dharma wanted a supply of T-shirts like the one she was wearing. On the front it said "Inner Peace, World Peace" and on the back "Keep on Meditating." She asked me to find out from Anna how many to order and in what sizes and colors. I went off to find Anna, seeing in my mind's eye a shrimp boat with a crew of burly tattooed men wearing sleeveless T-shirts bearing slogans about beer and motorcycles, and Roy among them in a shirt that said "Keep on Meditating"—bright blue, the color of his eyes. I took Anna's order to Cheri and added one extra-large in blue. I did it almost without thinking, then forgot it.

Roy stayed clear of the dormitory, and none of us saw him except at meals and meditation. His efforts at dinner-table conversation were minimal and involved what appeared to be strenuous attempts to suppress anger. But after the first time we meditated together, he surprised us by initiating a discussion with Cheri. How, he asked, could egocentricity be gotten rid of?

"It's not something to be gotten rid of," Cheri said. "It is to be embraced."

Roy looked at her steadily, and she looked back.

"Egocentricity is suffering, which is the same as the illusion of separateness," she continued. "Egocentricity is that which experiences itself as separate from all that is, and because of that, it suffers. For some people, it is helpful to see egocentricity in terms of subpersonalities. Subpersonalities are aspects of ourselves. I like to talk about them as children who are frightened, upset, hurt, and are getting more and more agitated in trying to defend themselves. Seeing them that way makes it easier to want to bring them into our hearts. If we look at a part of ourselves, like rage or violence, as some huge, hideous thing, then we want to get rid of it. But if we see it as a child who has been injured, it's a little harder to turn away. It is a matter of embracing, not killing, the ego."

The path of ending suffering, she said, requires only that you accept that which is most unacceptable to you. You don't have to do a single thing to improve yourself. All you have to do is embrace the suffering in this imperfect person.

"Only egocentricity would want to make you a perfect person. We suffer as long as we're trying to do something that cannot be done, and since we'll never be perfect, the process of suffering can be endless. So the most helpful first step is to stop inflicting additional suffering, stop being hard on ourselves. No matter what you did, thought, or said, no beating yourself up about it."

Roy spoke hoarsely. "What do you do . . . instead?"

"Let me tell you about my five-year-old grandson," Cheri replied. "He is one of the world's all-time adorable human beings. He can also be a little devil, and now and then, I confess, I have fantasies of throttling him. I just might beat him if I thought it would help, but I know it won't. So when I consider how to be with him and who I would like him to be twenty-five years from now, I know what I need to do is *be* the person I would like *him* to be in the world: loving and compassionate and gentle and happy and peaceful."

Roy just kept looking at her.

"The same is true with us," Cheri said. "Whatever it is that I don't like about what I am being, doing, or feeling will never be resolved by hating it and beating it. That just keeps the struggle going. But when part of me does its worst, and all it meets with is compassion—well, there's kind of nowhere for it to go with that. And so the struggle is over."

"Are you enlightened?" Roy asked Cheri.

"If you are traveling in unknown territory, you do well to consult someone who's been there," she said quietly. "That's all I am: a guide on this particular path. It's important to remember that this path has no end. It's not as if you get somewhere and then you can stop. This is a practice you follow every moment. I am walking the path myself, and so I am able to point out that you also are on the path, and that your only problem is that you don't know it."

Roy said he planned to spend some time alone in the mountains when he left Southern Dharma, and he suspected that something momentous was going to happen to him then. He wanted to know from Cheri whether it would be dangerous to be alone in the wilderness if he was struck by enlightenment.

"Not at all," she said softly. "There is absolutely nothing to be afraid of."

That may be so, but I was still afraid of Roy. Cheri spent one morning working with Roy on making drawers, and after lunch she told me she had learned he was a Vietnam veteran and that he had been unable to settle down after he got back from the war. What I had heard about posttraumatic stress syndrome did nothing to allay my apprehension.

Late that afternoon, when I had a few minutes free before supper, I walked up the road toward the spot where Anna's house had been. When I reached the barn, Roy was sitting in the doorway, holding a handful of wildflowers.

"Hi," he said, smiling awkwardly. "I've been wanting to ask somebody . . ."

He got up and walked to where I stood in the road. "Would it be all right to take these flowers to meditation? I was thinking I might put them in front of where I sit. I don't much like facing that blank wall." He made an effort to laugh.

To my surprise, I did not laugh nervously in response, or spout reassurances. I said nothing at first, I simply regarded his question. Then I heard myself answer, more simply and thoughtfully than usual. "There's no reason not to take them in. There aren't any rules about it. No one would object."

"Oh, well, uh . . . good. Because I thought it might help my concentration to have something to focus my mind on, you know. The kind of meditation I learned, you concentrate on something. Candle flame or flowers or something."

We stood for some moments. I was not thinking, but waiting—to see what I would say. When the words came, I listened with genuine interest.

"The kind of meditation the people here practice isn't just concentration. Cheri could tell you more about techniques. But whatever technique you use, I think the point is to be still enough to notice what happens in your mind, to get to know how your mind works. Sort of just being with yourself, in a gentle way. So if you would like to follow the practice we're doing, you might try that. Then we'll all be talking about the same thing in the discussions."

"Oh, yeah, okay. Hey, thanks," he said.

Then an anxious discomfort came over me, and I felt the need to strike up a conversation. I asked how he had become interested in meditation.

"When I was in the Angola . . . " he began.

"Angola?"

"You know, the prison in Louisiana. My cellmate was this Jap. He was some sort of Buddhist, I guess, and he used to tell me about meditation."

I do not know what I replied, surely nothing that required waiting and listening for a still, small voice. My mind was fully occupied with what Roy might have done to get sent to jail, but I didn't want to find out while I was alone with him. I made an excuse, turned back down the road, and headed to my room. Cheri was coming down the hall, her arms stacked with T-shirts. I asked if we could talk; I said I thought Roy was dangerous.

"Would you like to do a little projection exercise?" Cheri asked, heading to her room and motioning to me to follow. "It's relevant, I promise."

I agreed, and we sat down opposite each other on the bunk beds. Cheri began by asking me what it was about Roy that made me afraid. I said I thought he was crazy. She pressed me to be specific. He is so intense, I said, so disconnected from other people. She asked if I could see those qualities in myself.

At first I felt defensive, but I tried to consider the question honestly. Yes, I admitted, I could be intense. And while I did not *think* I was disconnected from other people, sometimes . . . yes, when it was brought to my attention that I was being "too intense," wasn't that a euphemism for behaving in a way that could be called disconnected? I was aware that people were put off by that quality in me. And I had to admit that disconnection was something I feared, so much that I couldn't bear to think about it.

Cheri nodded.

A strange notion: that I looked at Roy, saw my own tendencies, and felt afraid. It turned things inside out. The idea of projection seemed a little less improbable.

Cheri asked if I would like to take our exploration a little further. Again I agreed. She suggested that I allow myself to feel the fear. It took some effort—or rather, letting go of the effort *not* to feel fear, the effort that went into talking about it instead. After a few moments, I was able to experience that gnawing sensation in my chest that means "scared."

"Now," said Cheri, "see if you can visualize the part of you, the subpersonality, who is feeling the fear."

I saw in my mind's eye a dark, unformed being, tense and cringing, child sized but not quite human. I described it to her.

"Ask it to tell you about the fear."

An imaginary conversation ensued in which the being spoke about feeling isolated and different from other people, fearing their contempt and rejection.

"How do you feel toward this part of yourself?" Cheri prompted.

"Well . . . I feel terribly sad and want to do something to help. But I also feel . . . revulsion, hatred, even."

"Can you see who feels the revulsion?"

A tall woman appeared in my mind, stern and authoritarian. She wanted nothing to do with the wretched child.

"You've just encountered another subpersonality," Cheri said. "There are lots of them, and they all need attention. But for now, why don't you ask this grown-up one to wait until you have time to get to know her better and go back to the child."

The scene changed like a movie in my mind. Cheri asked if I could comfort the child, but it recoiled from me.

"That's all right," she said. "Just be there with it."

In my imagination, I approached that fearful part of myself the way one would a wild animal, by not approaching at all. Being still. Being patient. Waiting. Allowing its fear to subside, making no attempt to overcome the separateness. Eventually recognizing that we are as much together as apart. Nothing else needing to happen. The bare acceptance of what is, and knowing that the acceptance itself is compassion.

I told Cheri what I saw. She asked if I thought I could be with Roy in the same way.

It was hard to imagine, but my aversion had softened. I did feel some connection with him through my own fear. If he felt as different, as isolated, as threatened as that child in me did, how could I not feel sympathy for him?

"Remember that we do not know what's going on with Roy," Cheri cautioned me. "Maybe he was in jail because he is an ax murderer. Maybe he wrote a bad check. Maybe he's a political dissident and will become a hero. Maybe he'll get enlightened when he leaves here and become a saint. We don't know. But you've just learned something about *you*, and perhaps that will make it easier to be around him. To be with *yourself* around him, that is."

I recounted for Cheri my talk with Roy about bringing the flowers into the meditation hall. "I wasn't afraid then. I heard myself telling him about meditation, things I didn't know that I knew. And what I heard coming from myself was so simple and clear and kind—just the right thing to say in that situation."

Cheri nodded. "My teacher used to say, 'You will do for the love of others what you will not do for yourself.'"

That embarrassed me. I did not feel love for Roy. And I did not like thinking of the things I would not do for myself, starting with being patient about meditation.

"I don't know where all that came from," I insisted. "It wasn't at all like me—"

"But it *was* you, and so are all the other parts you're beginning to see and get to know," Cheri said. "But now let's take care of these T-shirts." She consulted a list. "You ordered one extra-large in blue, right? Here it is." She handed the shirt to me and bowed.

I went to my room, tossed the T-shirt onto a shelf, and lay down to think over the experience with subpersonalities. Although it had taken place in my imagination, it seemed very real. Or maybe not "real" so much as "true"—truer than much of what went on in regular life.

That night, a bunch of wildflowers appeared in a jar on the table at the front of the meditation hall. I felt a twinge of regret that I was not the one who had found the courage to put flowers there. It was clear what had inhibited me: fear—of doing something inappropriate in the eyes of others.

Roy's flowers were a bit weedy looking, and one fern frond had already gone limp, drooping down the side of the jar. A far cry from the plastic excesses of the Buddhist Temple altars, with their statues and colored lights and artificial flowers. And yet, in both of those, I sensed something that I always seemed to hold back from: simple sincerity.

During the next few days, Roy seemed a little more relaxed. I was not at ease around him, but at least I did not try to avoid him.

I was washing dishes when the sliding panel between the kitchen and the dining room rattled. Huge, rough, red fingers slipped underneath and raised the panel from the other side. Roy stuck his head through and managed something like a smile.

"Tell me something nice," he said.

"What?" Fear in my chest choked any intelligent response.

"Just say something nice to me. I need to hear something nice."

"I . . . I can't think of anything right now." Then my panic provided me with an escape. "But . . . actually, I've got something for you. Wait here."

I flew out of the kitchen and up to my room, as if I were being chased. It crossed my mind to simply stay there, since Roy considered the dormitory off-limits. But I grabbed the T-shirt and tore back downstairs.

"Here," I said, holding it out to him.

He looked unnerved and made no move to take the shirt.

"It's for you."

"For me?"

"Yes."

"Really, for me?" No . . ."

"Yes, it is. Please, take it."

Hesitantly, he accepted the shirt. "Why?"

"Oh, I liked the idea of you wearing a meditation T-shirt on a shrimp boat. Spread the word, you know."

He held the shirt awkwardly and kept his eyes lowered.

The silence felt unbearable. "I thought this color . . ." I began, then stopped.

"Thanks," he muttered, without looking at me.

I ran up to my room and lay on my bunk, shaking inside. Not with fear, I noted, but from sheer social discomfort. I didn't know how, or who, to be with Roy.

In a few minutes, I heard the downstairs door open and close, and I looked out the window. Roy was walking toward the barn. Flashing across his back against the bright blue ground was "Keep on Meditating."

The next morning, I was on my way to the meditation hall when I encountered Roy coming up the dormitory stairs. It didn't register with me that that was odd. He said something about a different space, but I didn't catch it, so I just nodded and kept going.

At meditation, there were only Cheri, Anna, Joel, and me. Shortly after we began to sit, a car started up. The silence was filled with the sound of it rolling on gravel, out of the parking lot and up and out of the cove. When we came outside afterward, the big red car was gone. Over breakfast, we talked quietly about Roy. I felt puzzled, saddened, hoping he would be all right, wherever he was headed.

When I went back to my room, something on the windowsill caught my eye. It was a tiny, perfect, fiery red-orange seahorse, not yet bleached by the sun.

CHAPTER 11

THE FIFTH HINDRANCE

THE TEACHER REFUSES TO SUPPORT EGO'S SCHEMES.

I liked to think of myself as still following the vipassana tradition of meditation that I had learned at the retreats in Nashville and with Achan Sobin. Certainly I did not see myself as a Zen student. I planned to use the overtime I was accumulating at Southern Dharma to sit an upcoming vipassana retreat, which was conveniently far in the future.

In vipassana, there are names for everything. Any difficulty in meditation is bound to be caused by one of the Five Hindrances: Restlessness, Doubt, Torpor, Anger, Desire. I seemed to be making my way through them one by one. At that time, I was working on Restlessness. A year before it had been Doubt, which had disappeared without my noticing it. Restlessness proved so enduring, however, that it seemed unlikely that I would ever get around to Torpor. In my life off the cushion, Anger flared but subsided quickly. Desire I never thought about.

One thing I feared about Zen was the absence of such labels, which raised in my mind an ominous suggestion of the Great Void, Ultimate Emptiness. When Joel urged me to sit Cheri's work-meditation retreat, I hesitated. Cheri was an inspiring teacher and a regular person to boot, but Zen wasn't my style. On the other hand, Joel's suggestion was attractive. I could spend mornings, he said, as a regular retreatant, taking an assigned task for the hour of "working meditation" and use the longer afternoon work period to keep up with my staff job. Having part of the day for my regular routine—a retreat from the retreat—meant I would be less likely to get lost in the emptiness of hour upon hour of meditation. With mixed feelings, I decided to do it.

On the way to the meditation hall the first evening, I noticed a man sitting on the steps and scratching a fat, scruffy, tiger-striped cat, who nudged his legs. The man's forearms were so big that they made me think of Popeye. With dark eyes and a wide black mustache, wearing loose cotton trousers, a faded sweatshirt with the sleeves torn out, and a colorful braided band around one wrist, he looked like a cross between a Mexican revolutionary, a truck driver, and a rock star. It took effort not to stare.

At that introductory session, Cheri requested that we extend our practice of silence to "custody of the eyes," meaning not looking at each other. Instead, she asked us to offer ourselves and our fellow retreatants the privilege of pursuing spiritual practice undisturbed. If, in the course of working together, it was necessary to communicate, we would bow first and then, keeping eyes lowered, whisper only what was necessary. The purpose of working meditation is to practice maintaining mindfulness while engaged in activity, she said, and it's important to remember that our spiritual training is ultimately for living life in the ordinary world. This retreat, she told us, would be more like regular life in that we would spend more time working than sitting. Also, there would be a certain amount of coming and going, because people who were not able to attend a full retreat were participating in this one as their schedules permitted.

Cheri began making the work assignments by asking who had experience operating a chain saw. The man with the Popeye arms raised his hand. A woman on the other side of the room raised her hand too. Cheri asked the man to speak with Anna about sawing a large tree trunk into firewood. Resentment stirred in me; I thought she should have let the woman do it.

I had my own assignment to think about, though. Telling myself that Zen meant accepting everything with equanimity, I had braced myself for the spiritual opportunity of getting a job I did not want, which was anything indoors. Yet a small, unseemly wish escaped into my consciousness: that I be assigned to rake leaves from the ditch along the road. It would not only require a short walk and moderate exercise, but it might also aid a cause in which I had become intensely inter-ested, building a compost heap. Just this once, I thought, after weeks of office work, the spirit might benefit from a small reward such as having this wish granted.

When all the jobs were matched with people, Cheri turned to me. "Would you rake the leaves from the ditch along the road?"

Me? I wanted to say. But that's exactly what . . . I *want* to do!

✧　✧　✧

At the first work period, I walked to the toolshed to get a rake and shovel, as instructed in the handwritten note describing the job. I was rummaging through the box of work gloves, looking for an unmildewed matched pair, when the tiger cat appeared. Behind the cat came the man with the Popeye arms who had changed into overalls and work boots. I glanced surreptitiously at his dark eyes and eyebrows and straight black hair. He took the chain saw down, then strapped on a yellow hard hat and goggles. As he left the toolshed, I stared, flagrantly disregard-ing the guideline about keeping custody of the eyes.

Now that it was forbidden, looking at people became a major source of pleasure. As I had at the Buddhist Temple, I devised strategies that allowed me to indulge the urge to observe my surroundings, in this case, the other retreatants. The first strategy, which I called Neck Down, interpreted "lowered eyes" to mean that I could stare at anything below people's faces. This enabled me to produce an extensive mental catalog of retreat fashion, moving upward from sandals and clogs and running shoes through jeans, khakis, long skirts, harem pants, sweatpants, flannel shirts, T-shirts, scarves, shawls, and, occasionally, the edge of a Duofold undershirt riding up a neck. The second strategy, Eyes Only, permitted observation during walking meditation of whatever was visible if I faced straight ahead but allowed my eyes to roam. This was based on the premise that no one would be looking backward to witness my staring (although simple logic nagged me with the awareness that just as I could see those ahead in the arc of the circle, so could those behind see me). I had redefined "custody of the eyes" to suit my interests, and, in contemplating this trick I was playing on myself, I recognized the feeling that prompted the looking as none other than desire.

I shouldered the tools, lowered my gaze, and walked out of the shed to the road. Would looking at other people count as Desire, one of the Five Hindrances to spiritual practice? Surely desire for visual pleasure was less likely to cause harm than the kind of desire we usually mean. I put it out of my mind.

The sound of hammering came from the sauna, and a wheelbarrow clattered toward the garden. The chain saw sputtered into action in the distance. I listened with longing. I had the job I wanted, but now it felt lonely. Everyone else was toiling in happy if silent camaraderie, while I was trudging farther and farther away from the center of things.

At the top of the hill, I pushed my desolate feeling aside and attempted to focus on my job. My note said to rake leaves loose from the narrow ditch beside the road, drag them across to the other side, and fling them down the hill. Rake, drag, fling. Rake, drag, fling. In some places, the leaves were covered with a layer of clay, which required the shovel. In other places, the ditch disappeared. At times it was all very interesting, which is to say, I was absorbed in it.

Absorbed: a good word for the experience. But those moments were interspersed with various forms of dissatisfaction, mostly craving, for that is what it had become, for the company of others. My thoughts focused mainly on the chainsawer in the hard hat, the Popeye man, as I had begun to call him.

About twenty yards along, I came to a tree that leaned menacingly over the ditch. It needed attention; an operation by chain saw would be my recommendation. I considered whether it would be more appropriate to act as a retreatant or a staff member in this matter. I thought about it off and on all afternoon and evening, and I did not sleep well that night.

The next day, at the beginning of the first work period, I headed toward the toolshed with the intention of suggesting to the wielder of the chain saw—bowing properly first, of course—that the leaning tree be dealt with as soon as he had finished with his present task. Naturally, I would show him where it was, even discuss it with him, in a discreet whisper, bending our heads close together . . .

I was waiting (lurking, actually) in the dimness, watching out through the cracks of the shed to see him come up the road, when to my dismay, I saw Cheri approaching. She entered purposefully, as if aware of my presence. Indeed, she appeared to be tracking me down. She bowed. I bowed in return.

"We need extra copies of the schedule for the kitchen and for the dormitory," she said. "Would you print them out and post them?"

I bowed.

"And one person has come down with the flu. Would you check in the second dorm room on the left and see if anything is needed?"

I bowed again.

On my way to the office, I saw the yellow hard hat heading toward the toolshed.

After I had made the copies and checked on the sick person, I walked back up the road and resumed clearing the ditch where I had left off, at the overhanging tree. For most of the remainder of the work period, I fretted about Cheri interrupting my plan. I even worried that she might be able to read my mind.

By the next day, my interest in the Popeye man had intensified to obsession. After much agonizing, I gave in to the impulse to approach him. I left the ditch before the gong rang for the next sitting and strode down toward the sound of the chain saw and the glimpse of bright yellow through the trees. Across the distance I studied the overalled figure bent toward a log, admiring the grace, the ease, the strength, the unselfconsciousness.

As I walked closer, I realized that something was not right about the way the body inhabited the overalls. The boots were not right, either. This was not the figure of my fantasy. I saw a fringe of auburn under the hard hat and a slim, pale wrist. The woman who knew how to handle a chain saw was doing just that.

I suspected Cheri of having deliberately arranged it to unsettle me. I was annoyed and confused. During lunch, I rationalized my concern about the Popeye man not being at his assigned job—as a staff member, shouldn't I check to see if there was some problem? As he left the dining room, I was a few paces behind, trying to ignore the peripheral sense of a small but energetic black presence dogging my steps.

Outside, the Popeye man stopped to tie his boot. I wavered in my purpose, and the black figure caught up with me.

Cheri bowed and whispered. "Some new people are coming and want to sit the rest of the retreat. Would you help me round up four more cushions and rearrange the seating in the hall so they can be accommodated?"

I bowed. We walked silently to the library, picked up two cushions each, took them to the meditation hall, and lined them up in the back. I was halfway out the door when a tug on my sleeve reminded me to bow before leaving the hall. I turned, we both faced the front of the room, and as Cheri's head went down, I thought I saw a little smile.

I could not sleep again that night. What did I want? Was this another form of Restlessness, or was it actually Desire? I thought of monastics struggling with temptations of the flesh, the fires of passion. I tried to pay attention to what I was experiencing. It sure felt like fire.

The next day, I decided to put the Hindrances out of mind and focus again on work. As I passed the overhanging tree, I choked back the hot, resentful voice that cried within me, "Let it fall, let it block the road, let it hit a car! I tried to tell them, but no one would listen."

Rake, drag, fling. Rake, drag, fling. I practiced synchronizing my breath with my movements, getting it all together in some sort of oneness. Very Zen, I thought.

After a while, I remembered my interest in using all those leaves for compost. Anna could bring the truck up, I would throw the leaves in the back, and we would dump them near the garden site. I shouldered my tools and went to tell Anna my brilliant idea.

Cheri was sitting in one of the two lawn chairs below the meditation hall with the tiger cat in her lap. She motioned to me to join her. If I wanted to have a quick guidance interview, she offered, we could do it right then before the next sitting.

I did not have the courage to say no. At a loss for something to discuss, I once again described my poor concentration.

She nodded. "It may seem that way, but in fact, every moment, the awareness is there. The still, small voice. It seems as if it's only there sometimes, that most of the time it's gone. But . . ."

Yes, yes, I thought, I've heard this before.

Cheri looked at me pointedly. "But it's *you* who are gone."

Where? I almost said, irritated and frustrated. Then I saw how, during the past few days, the raging of my mind, a roaring chain saw of my own creation, drowned out any still, small voice. I did not *want* to hear the still, small voice.

"Well, maybe I see that," I said, nodding ruefully.

Not wishing to pursue the subject further, I shifted roles from student to staff member and informed Cheri of my plan to enlarge on the usefulness of my work assignment by bringing the leaves down for compost. I spoke of natural cycles and mindless waste and the ease with which this project could be accomplished.

Cheri pointed out that Anna was using the truck to haul firewood. I presented reasons for postponing that and hauling the leaves for compost right away, asserting the rightness, even righteousness of my position. Cheri listened and nodded and proposed that I consult the still, small voice on the question.

During the sitting period that followed, I felt guilty about walking away from my work assignment (not to mention chagrined at being caught). I accused myself of having manufactured the compost project as an excuse to escape the monotony of the same job and to get to talk to somebody. In an abject mood, I resolved not only to strictly follow the schedule for sitting and walking and working but also to volunteer for any extra work that needed to be done and to keep absolutely silent. At first I intended that regimen partly as self-punishment, but then I began to see it as a major insight: it is so simple—just be perfect.

At lunch, Anna asked for someone to ring the gong during the afternoon, and I volunteered. I made the rounds, solemnly striking the gong ten minutes before the first afternoon sitting. Then, convinced that I was finally making spiritual progress, I rushed to the meditation hall, eager to get to my cushion.

On the way, I was intercepted by Cheri, who whispered that more people had arrived. Would I meet them in the library and explain everything they needed to know, then bring them to the hall for the walking period? I did not like being deflected from my plan, but I was pleased to be asked and saw the interruption as a challenge to my resolve, an opportunity to be better than ever. Puffed with importance, the ego was all too happy to switch from irritation to acceptance. I bowed and went back down the hill.

While showing the new people the schedule, I noticed that the next gong was due to be rung halfway through the walking period. It made no sense. I directed the newcomers to the meditation hall and went to look for Joel. When I couldn't find him, I assumed that the time was a misprint. But the gong ringer's job is to follow the schedule, not to question it, I could imagine Cheri saying. I would feel foolish ringing the gong at the wrong time; on the other hand, I certainly did not want to foul up things by neglecting to ring it when it was expected. Perfection was proving elusive.

By then, the walking had begun. I decided against the gong. If I interrupted the walking, I would be blamed, whereas no gong would be blamed on whomever was responsible for the error on the schedule.

To renew my resolution to be extra good, I decided to use the time remaining in the walking period to return to my job and rake more leaves. On the way to the toolshed, I saw the orange pickup truck halfway off the road below the meditation hall, its nose and front wheels hanging over the edge of a bank. A red tow truck was rumbling and clanking toward it across the clearing.

A near disaster. I wanted to watch. Who wouldn't?

Around the porch of the meditation hall, very slowly, came the little figure in black leading the silent line of retreatants, eyes downcast, faces impassive, taking their little Zen half-steps. How they must be dying to look down at the two trucks!

I moved one of the lawn chairs just under the edge of the porch, where no one could see me from above. Ah—a ringside view of the trucks. The tiger cat waddled up and sat at my feet, its ragged ears perked toward the action below.

Two men got out of the tow truck, and Anna walked over to them.

Above me, the retreatants stepped slowly, softly, silently. Looking directly overhead, I could see their feet through the planks of the porch. Step, step, step, like a giant millipede, all the left feet, then all the right, moving in unison.

The towing apparatus was hooked up. Anna got in the truck, and one of the men started the tow truck while the other signaled directions.

Now, *there* was something easy to pay attention to: a red truck rescuing an orange truck from a precipitous perch. The orange truck was pulled back onto the road, then the tow truck unhooked, and both trucks rumbled and clanked down the hill.

Just beyond the bridge over the creek, a motorcycle stopped to let the trucks pass. It must have coasted down from the ridge. I watched as it rolled quietly into the parking lot.

A man and woman removed their helmets and extricated two small black bags from the gear strapped on the back. They blew into the bags as they walked toward the meditation hall. By the time they reached the steps up to the porch, the bags were fully inflated, assuming the unmistakable shape of meditation cushions. Above me, the walkers were busy taking off their shoes and going back inside. The two new arrivals followed them, and inside the hall, the bell sounded for the next sitting.

I was gripped by strong feeling, at once sad and happy. Sitting in the chair watching the scene before me felt more real than anything I had experienced in days. And I was not making myself do anything: it just happened—me sitting there, meditators walking above, trucks fighting gravity, motorcycle arriving, cushions being inflated. The ordinary and the extraordinary alike, utterly absorbing. No good and bad and punishment and perfection and striving and avoiding.

I felt like running down to get the gong and striking it again and again and again, for the sheer joy of it, right in the middle of the sitting period. Instead, I sat very still, as still as the cat at my feet, my heart overflowing.

Another series of scenes passed through my mind: my intentions to act out various desires during the retreat, and how they were repeatedly short-circuited by Cheri. Whether her appearances at precisely those moments were calculated or accidental, I did not know. Now I would say that they were skillful actions taken on a purely intuitive level. Whatever their nature, I was grateful for those interventions. Thus was I rescued, like the orange truck, from the brink—no drama, no fuss, just a slight tug uphill, against the downward drag of life's gravity, the ego. It was then that I realized I had found my teacher.

CHAPTER 12

BEFORE THE BEGINNING OF
BEGINNINGLESS TIME

**FIT REGULAR LIFE INTO SPIRITUAL PRACTICE,
NOT THE OTHER WAY AROUND.**

Spring had arrived at full tilt. The pastels of flowering fruit trees and daffodils gave way to the vivid green of new leaves. Cheri's month at Southern Dharma was almost over.

After the last retreat, Joel proposed that the four of us go out to dinner. Getting away from Southern Dharma for an evening would be good for us, Cheri agreed, an opportunity to confront the perennial postretreat question of how you take spiritual practice into regular life.

My time at Southern Dharma was also coming to an end. And if our visit to the rafting center and Roy's visit to us, not to mention my reaction to the Popeye man, were any indication of what I was in for back in the "real world," I knew I had better take advantage of any opportunities for gradual readjustment. Anna suggested that we go to an inn up the road. Vegetarian meals were served family style in an old, quiet dining room, and the level of sociability would be manageable.

Twilight darkened into night as we wound along a creek and over a gap, then into the town and up a steep drive to the inn. Below us, I could see two traffic lights, a scatter of illuminated signs, and yellow windows opening into the warm interiors of living rooms and dining rooms and kitchens. The blink and flash and glow seemed to embody all the enchantments of civilization.

I remember sitting together around the big old table, four of us from the retreat center, a hiker who was staying at the inn, and the innkeeper, passing platters heaped with unexpected combinations of vegetables and grains, bowls of exotic sauces, a big colorful salad, a basket of homemade breads. Candlelight caressed our circle of faces, which were flushed with the pleasures of companionship.

Joel observed that the hiker had come from a lot of solitude and silence, just as we had.

"Yeah, when I'm walking the trail, it can get pretty meditative," the hiker said. "It's like I'm not making myself walk anymore, it's just happening, and there's this incredible stillness. Also, I'm reading this." He reached into his vest pocket and retrieved half a paperback copy of D. T. Suzuki's *Introduction to Zen Buddhism*.

"Ah, Suzuki is where I started, too," Cheri said. "But I had a whole book, which could be an advantage."

"Well, I'd read the first half and didn't want to carry any extra weight," the hiker explained. "I think this half will last me all the way to Maine. It's pretty slow going. The book, that is. I have to reread a lot of it."

Cheri laughed. "I know exactly what you mean."

The hiker said there was a lot he would like to discuss with a Zen teacher, things he had been thinking about on the trail. "There are these internal stories going on, you know. I've noticed that the things that feel most urgent are those that have the strongest emotions attached to them," he said.

"It's interesting that we think we need a story to justify what we're experiencing," Cheri said. "If we have a good enough story, we think it will be okay to feel what we're feeling. Why not just let it be okay to feel what we're feeling?

That would be easier. However, often we don't know what we're feeling without the story."

The hiker looked puzzled. "But the feeling wouldn't be there if the story hadn't happened."

"But something is there. Something triggered that story," Cheri said.

"Well . . . that's an interesting twist," Anna said slowly. "It's almost like you're saying the result comes before—"

"Remember," said Cheri, "when we talk about our karmic conditioning, we are talking in terms of 'before the beginning of beginningless time.' It's not as if this stuff all started last week."

There was a baffled silence.

Finally, Joel said, "So what's the best attitude to have? We're not going to unravel that knot, all our past karma."

"No reason not to," said Cheri. "However, there's also no reason to continue to suffer while we do it. It's like the story the Buddha told about the guy who's been shot with an arrow. He's lying there on the ground bleeding, and nobody's going to pull the arrow out until they know who he is and what he's doing there and where the arrow came from, by which time he would be very dead. It's much better just to pull the arrow out. Then if you want to know all those things, there's plenty of time later to find out."

The innkeeper slipped out and quickly returned with hot corn bread. The hiker had stopped eating and appeared to be stuck in thought.

Cheri continued. "So, no, we don't need to start before the beginning of beginningless time to resolve what's going on now. However, sometimes it's helpful to consider that much of what we're experiencing is simply karmic. Some of it you are personally involved with; much of it you are not. We want to make everything so very personal—that's just how we are. So a feeling comes along and we have to make it part of our story.

Again, the point is not to assume that the way it appears is necessarily the way it is."

"But if we see something ourselves," Anna said, "and that's our experience, how can it not be what it seems?"

"Well, for example, almost everybody believes that they get angry because somebody else does something they don't like. And it does seem that way. But when you look closely, that's not the way it works."

"If you mean that the anger originates in yourself, then why don't you project it onto everybody instead of just certain people?" Anna asked.

"Ah, because you are *you*, and you're looking at the world through the eyes of egocentricity, constantly deciding what in particular threatens you, what supports you. This is good, this is bad, I like this, I don't like that. This kind of person makes me mad, that kind doesn't. It may be completely different for somebody else. The entire universe is your mirror. Everything you experience, every moment of your life, is you."

"I'm having trouble with that," the hiker put in. "I'd like to get to the place where I could see clearly what someone does, and if it's destructive, take action if necessary—but without judging them."

Cheri leaned forward and spoke softly. "Well, I am all in favor of passing judgment—as long as you never forget who you're talking about."

"You mean, if you realize that you yourself are capable of these things?" Joel said.

"Exactly. That it's *my* experience, *my* perception. It may not be true for that other person at all."

"On the other hand, it may be true for them," I said.

"It may be. But that's their problem. You see, with projection, that's the wonderful part of it: we never really know for sure." She laughed. "But we do know that the experience is true for one person, the one who's seeing it and saying it.

Judging, if you pay attention to it, is an opportunity for you to see how you operate, to see that part of yourself. Once we realize that our experience of everything is all our own, we're looking in the right direction."

We filled the gaps in our comprehension by passing dishes around and helping ourselves to seconds. What Cheri said often seemed the opposite of common sense, and I marveled that the two outsiders took her seriously. Indeed, their questions were as earnest as any retreatant's, and they listened as intently to her answers. The same thing that had happened at the rafting center was happening at the inn: instead of Cheri fading into a more ordinary sort of being in the outside world, she became even more extraordinary. Later, I might have described that impression in terms of her being so fully present to the situation. At the time, I was speechless, fully caught up in watching the phenomenon. In fact, I myself was as fully present as I had ever been to anything.

The hiker asked how love fit into it all. He described the feeling of happiness in the presence of his girlfriend, being strongly drawn to her, caring about her intensely, the specialness of such a relationship.

Cheri asked if he could see how that idea of love relates to egocentricity, the sense we all have of our self as separate from everything else. Egocentricity, she reminded us again, is the source of suffering.

"It is certainly true that we will be drawn to particular people," she said, "for all sorts of reasons, the best one being that we simply enjoy their presence. But there is something else we might call love. Once we stop suffering, we exist in a state of love for everyone. Everything. Equally."

"Is that state the same as the True Self?" Joel asked.

Cheri nodded.

"If it's the *true* self, then what keeps us from being in that state all the time?" Anna said.

"Conditioning," Cheri answered. "Egocentricity. That's what we are trying to see through."

"I don't know much about Zen," the innkeeper said, "but it worries me to think about egolessness. Wouldn't losing your ego cause problems with functioning in the world—relating to other people, holding a job, that sort of thing?"

We all looked at Cheri. She laughed, a slightly wicked gleam in her eye, and spoke softly.

"There are those who maintain that people in my line of work shouldn't be allowed out by themselves. In the case of my own very dear teacher, there have been moments when I might have agreed. In my case, though," she whispered slyly, "I've noticed that I seem to be able to pass, in polite society and otherwise."

Joel, who was unfailingly polite, laughed almost hysterically. What amused him, it seemed, was the implication that society could be divided along lines such as polite and impolite. I figured he was having a miniexperience of nonseparateness.

Anna asked what made it so hard to take spiritual practice back into the world.

"It's not hard at all," Cheri said. "When you go to work, do spiritual practice at work. When you're with your family, do spiritual practice with your family. When you're playing, do spiritual practice. If spiritual practice is important to you, you simply do what's necessary to put it at the center of your life. Now, we've eliminated that difficulty. So what do you think is really going on with practicing and not practicing?"

"I guess for me it's willpower," Anna said. "Sort of like after you go to the dentist and get your teeth cleaned, the next week you floss every day. Then—well, your commitment tends to drop off."

Cheri said she was glad the subject of dentistry had come up, because one of her favorite ideas was that spiritual practice is like dental hygiene. "See if this isn't how it works for most of us. In the beginning, as small children, we are intro-duced to the notion of brushing our teeth. Right off, it does not appeal—unless you have the right toothpaste, in which case, eating toothpaste can be entertaining. But when that's no longer fun, it's a battle. Someone has to stand there and force you to do this tedious thing. Then we get to puberty, and another issue arises: being socially acceptable. So when-ever we're going somewhere important with someone impor-tant, we brush our teeth. The rest of the time, if we can get by without it, we do. This is the way we approach medita-tion, isn't it? But there comes a point when we're getting bad news from the dentist, and maybe there's another ingredient, pain, which is a great motivator. However, if we're tired, if it's late, if it's just too hard, we're still going to skip it. Later, we start paying our own dental bills, and eventually, adding up all those incentives, brushing our teeth is no longer an issue."

She's talking to me, I thought. She can see that as a medi-tator I am at the eating-toothpaste stage: wanting the magic of automatic, ever-after bliss, that sharp, minty-fresh, oh-so-clean blessing of the spirit but unwilling to accept the discipline of regular sitting meditation.

"We don't get up in the morning and have this big debate about whether we're going to brush our teeth," she was say-ing. "We just do it. When spiritual practice moves into that place in your life, the struggle is ended. You don't have to decide whether or not you like it. If you meditate only when you want to, you'll meditate very rarely. It has to move into the realm of willingness: willingness is what's there even when wanting to meditate isn't.

"Now, the whole point of spiritual training is taking behavior out of the area of wanting and not wanting. Wanting becomes irrelevant. Once we find the willingness, the decision is made from a much deeper place, and from that place it's clear: I am going to meditate. So it's not hard to take spiritual practice back into the world. You simply have to want to, and when you don't want to, you have to be willing."

Her voice dropped to her near-whisper. "Things are always going to be the way they are. When we wake up and see that, when we let go our resisting what is and suffering over it, we are free."

The words, the thought, the promise hung in the still space above the table.

❖ ❖ ❖

I thought about how I would say good-bye to Cheri. I wondered how to express my gratitude for what I had learned. But the next morning she was already gone. She left the way she had come: silently, invisibly, with no hellos, no good-byes, just gone.

Settling

In Silence: Working Meditation

I got the job I wanted. My assignment is to clean chairs.
Handwritten instructions specify how this is to be done:
wipe all surfaces thoroughly with a quarter cup of Murphy's
Oil Soap diluted in a gallon of water, then wipe with clean
rinse water and a nearly dry sponge. I work silently, carefully, as fully present as possible to the details of the task.

Yesterday I cleaned all the wooden chairs in the dining
hall. Once I got a rhythm going—dunk sponge in bucket,
squeeze, wipe, turn chair—it seemed as if the chair and I
were performing a dance step, and I had a great time.

The instructions are from the Work Director, a Zen
monk who coordinates the work activities of this ten-day
"working meditation" retreat. Twice a day, thirty Zen students troop into the area set aside as the Work Director's
center of operations, where cleaning supplies are assembled
with military precision atop a washer and dryer. Containers
of spray cleaner, glass cleaner, toilet bowl cleaner, scrubbing
powder, disinfectant, and Murphy's Oil Soap stand in rows
alongside orderly stacks of rags and sponges, scrub brushes,
and two kinds of rubber gloves. Next to the utility sink rest

plastic pails, rubber buckets, brooms, three kinds of mops, and a serious vacuum cleaner.

On the first evening, Cheri had explained the purpose of this kind of retreat. In "working meditation," the emphasis is on mindfulness, not on accomplishment. Learning to meditate while engaged in activity is an essential step in bringing fuller awareness to ordinary life, and our retreat offered an opportunity to practice that. No rushing to complete a task to savor the little ego burst of pride. No perfectionist striving, and, of course, no sloppiness, but the middle way of steady attentiveness. No questioning one's assignment or the instructions for carrying it out, but the calm acceptance one dreams of bringing to all of life. And what about when we catch ourselves rushing and striving and careless and critical, as no doubt we will? Then we simply notice that and return our attention to our work. Most of us have heard it all before; we have been attending such retreats for years. But habit dies hard, and we are here to practice, practice, practice the middle way.

Today my job is to clean plastic outdoor chairs. It is snowing. My workstation is under a roof, but the cold air bites into me. The rubber gloves I have were made for a giant, and no matter how careful I am, the icy water dribbles into them. I ponder whether it is worse to wear the gloves, which are holding the water in, or to plunge my bare hand into the bucket of water.

I keep the gloves on, and my hands really, really hurt. My resentment escalates. This is sadomasochism!

Off with the gloves. I slap them down onto a chair and march inside to the Work Director's station. I take a ballpoint pen and a piece of scrap paper from the stack provided. "My assignment . . ." I write, then scratch that out and write, "The weather is simply too cold. . . ." But the paper is too small (deliberately, I suspect) to contain my grievances. I wad it up and angrily throw it away.

Down the hall I see the Work Director heading in my direction, and Cheri is a few steps behind. Was my near-tantrum witnessed? Trying to look casual, I walk out and return to the plastic chairs.

The chairs became increasingly irksome. Their nether surfaces feature odd-shaped depressions with acute angles that are inaccessible to the human hand. Actually, the only things I see to be cleaned from these chairs are deep in the corners of those angles: occasional spongy white spheres I take to be spider egg sacs.

These chairs are not dirty! I say vehemently, if silently. And even if they were, anybody knows that the way to clean them is to just hose them down. And once the dirt works into the plastic—it says so right there on the bottom!—recycle. Why are we treating disposable stuff like Chippendale? This is craziness! What am I doing here?

Out of the corner of my eye, I see the Work Director approaching. A jumble of thoughts: Have I been working hard enough, or, rather, have I given the impression of doing so? No, no, that's not the point: have I been working mind-fully? Well, not today, not so far, but no excuses, no blame, no guilt. Just bring the attention back. . . .

The Work Director bows, hands me a note and a pair of gloves with extra-long cuffs, bows again, then leaves. The note says, "If your hands get too cold, you could go into the kitchen and fill your pail with hot water as often as you need to. And you might stop and drink a cup of tea to warm up. [signed] Work Director."

I have no idea who initiated this act of mercy—which of the two of them, I mean. I entertain suspicions of telepathy and/or spying (could they have sunk to retrieving my note from the trash?), along with breach of silence at high levels. Probably I will never know. But I do know that it came from pure kindness, and I'm touched.

Ten minutes later, I have returned to my task in a happy frame of mind, with a bucket of steaming water and my own wool gloves under the longer rubber gloves, which are pulled up securely over my sleeves. I find a twig just the right size to reach into the crevices in the chair bottoms and remove the spiders-in-waiting, which I carefully transport to a sheltered spot under the edge of the roof, as I know Cheri would do and would want me to do also. Then I wash the chairs.

These chairs don't do the dance of the wooden chairs. It doesn't work just to turn them this way and that. I have to bend over them; they want to be stroked, caressed . . . ah, I see—it is a different dance. The dining room chairs did a minuet, and these guys want to tango. My body begins to get a sense of this new rhythm.

I remember why I am here: to make my peace with the world, which so often is not as I would have it. I see, once again, how my suffering is self-imposed. I recognize yet another instance in which the result of Buddhist practice is intelligent action. And I recall that this path is about compassion.

In my years of looking for a spiritual path, I met teachers who knew more about Buddhism, teachers with impeccable pedigrees, teachers whose every gesture shone with virtue, teachers whose manner was gentler and who more closely matched my idea of a "Zen type." But I never met one who was more effective than Cheri in encouraging students to walk the path of compassion in ordinary life.

CHAPTER 13

EMPTY CUSHION

TO OPEN THE HEART, TURN THE STREAM
OF COMPASSION INWARD.

For a while after I left Southern Dharma, some of the experience stayed with me, especially a sort of freshness of perception. When I became aware of looking at something—a tree, usually, but it could be a house or an animal or anything else—I was struck by the sheer marvel of its being. That blessed state, which I told myself I must never lose, seemed to have arisen from the practice, however intermittent, of stillness and attentiveness. But while awareness of the miracle of a tree was a pleasant reminder of where I had come from, it did little to dispel my deeper habits of conditioning. Dissatisfactions rose again, crowding out the utter sufficiency of mere existence.

I decided to try freelance editing, partly because a more flexible work life would make it easier to attend retreats. A few months after I left Southern Dharma, before I had established any regular work, Anna telephoned. The summer retreat season had moved into full swing, she told me, and every weekend had seen a capacity crowd. The week before, flu had swept through the dormitory, taking its toll among retreatants and staff alike. Barely back on their feet and facing imminent burn-out, Anna and Joel needed some respite. Anna wondered if I would like to come for a week between retreats. I wouldn't be entirely alone—they would be in and out—but my handling the day-to-day business of mail and telephone would give them a break.

I was being offered a vacation in the mountains before I'd even done enough work to earn it, and without having to sit a retreat. Yes, I said, of course. I'd love to come.

❖ ❖ ❖

A group of retreatants was leaving when I arrived, and the parking lot was soon empty, except for one truck. I wondered who was still around.

I put my things up in the third-floor loft, a big, bright space with long skylight-windows in the southern slope of the roof, like those in the meditation hall. I opened the middle window, pulled a foam mattress under it, and made up my bed with extra blankets and pillows. I raided the library; its being declared off-limits during Cheri's retreats lent the alluring aura of forbidden fruit to such innocuous items as *Psychology of Meditation* and back issues of the *Buddhist Peace Fellowship Newsletter*. Up the ladder I carried a reading lamp and an extension cord. I was fired by the delicious idea of indulgence combined with freedom: reading in bed, tucked deep under a pile of covers, no rules, no schedule, and above me nothing but the night sky.

As Anna showed me the office work that needed to be done before the next retreat, my ambition shifted from spiritual to administrative achievement. "Don't feel you have to finish it all," Anna said, but already my mind had lurched ahead to the satisfaction of accomplishment: finishing it all was precisely what made work attractive.

Anna and I were standing at the refrigerator surveying the leftovers when the kitchen door swung inward, held wide by a bulging forearm. In hobbled the tiger-striped cat, followed by the Popeye man. I was suddenly conscious of wearing a messy, oversized apron.

"Hey, Annie!" he roared, opening his arms wide.

"Sidney, hey!" Anna responded, obviously delighted.

He gave her a big hug. Anna grinned and introduced us.

"Well, hey, there," he said. He placed his hands together at his chest and made an exaggerated bow. "Swami Sidananda at your service."

Then he stepped back, drew a giant red ballpoint pen from his back pocket, and, brandishing it like a baton, marched to the narrow desk below the wall telephone, where he tapped out a drumroll.

"Always from this place is disappearing any and all writing implements!"

For someone who seemed southern, Sidney managed a first-class Indian accent. He pulled a wad of cord from a pocket and proceeded to attach the pen to the desk. "So. Here I am bringing special pen, and affixing, you see, in very secure manner." He tugged on the string. "This pen is available now for writing down messages from telephone and from answering machine. Messages both sacred and profane. You must have some of both. This is swami's teaching for today." He bowed again.

We laughed. He laughed. I felt as if a rainbow had exploded in the room.

Sidney said he had been scouting around for a good place to build a new outhouse, to reduce overuse of indoor bathrooms, which caused plumbing problems during retreats. He and Anna sat on the kitchen stools and talked energetically about building plans. I opened the refrigerator door several times and looked in to see if I could remember what Anna and I had been doing. I wiped all the countertops, and I cleaned the soap dish on the sink. Then I picked up the tiger cat, rescuing it from imminent threat by Anna's big tom, and dropped all pretense of being usefully occupied.

When Sidney went to his truck to get a bag of cat chow, Anna told me about him.

"He shows up now and then and stays a few days. He can do anything: carpentry, plumbing, stonemasonry," she said. "He helped me build that stone wall by the entrance. He's a great cook, too. He just tells Joel to take a vacation from the kitchen, and we all have the guilty pleasure of enjoying gourmet meals instead of macrobiotic."

Sidney was a committed meditator, Anna said. Sometimes he sat in the hall the whole night, and she would see him doing walking meditation outside when she got up. Anna said she thought of him as a bodhisattva, because his whole drive and purpose in life seemed to be helping other people.

Something must have gotten cooked for supper. I remember taking off the apron and Sidney gesturing grandly toward the center table in the dining room, where the three of us sat down and ate.

I felt as if I'd been waiting all my life for someone else to take charge, so I would be relieved of always doing it myself, I guess. I was also waiting for someone to help me with meditation, and Sidney seemed to be the perfect person to consult about my difficulties. I described my sitting practice to him.

"So far, it seems like an endless series of erroneous preconceptions," I said.

"Let me guess: you started by aiming for total Cosmic Awareness." He opened his eyes wide and rolled them around.

"Well—"

"And when that didn't happen, you could only scale downward, right?"

"Yes . . ."

"So then you tried for Perfect One-Pointedness of Mind? And after that Deep Concentration? Then mere Steady Attentiveness? Hey, you might as well go all the way to 'just sitting'!"

Taking that to be a joke, I ignored it. "Now and then I get a glimpse of what sitting is all about," I explained, "but the problem is, I can't seem to maintain it."

"But that is the problem, isn't it?" Sidney said. "That's precisely why we sit. That's why it's called *practice!*"

After supper, Sidney and Anna went to look at the proposed site for the outhouse, saying they would meet me in half an hour for meditation. I headed upstairs to take a shower. When I got to the second floor, a leadenness hit me, and by the time I climbed to the loft and lay down, I was shaking with chills. It felt like the flu; in any case, I was through for the evening.

Several hours of fevered misery later, I broke into perspiration. Then I pulled off my damp nightgown, put on a sweatsuit, and finally slept. The next day I got up late. I managed to climb down to the second floor and wash my face, but I was too weak to make it down another flight of stairs to eat. I thought of the office work with dismay as I stumbled into the first dormitory room and collapsed on a bare bunk. I was half asleep when Sidney came in, carrying his cat and a book.

"I wish I'd known you were sick," he said. "I'd have been right here with hot tea and vitamin C and some of that herbal miracle powder they keep in the kitchen."

I pulled myself up and leaned against the wall. Sidney put the cat down beside me and sat on the opposite bunk. I thought about how with my dank hair and in my worn, faded sweatsuit, I must look rather like the cat—even to devoted admirers of the species, scarcely one of the finer examples. The cat purred hoarsely and pawed in my lap. Sidney opened the book, looked at me, then put the book down.

"Nourishment," he said decisively. "That's what you need. Don't move. It's on its way."

He strode out, whistling, and bounded down the stairs. I closed my eyes. A long, loud whirr came from the kitchen, and I drifted into the sound and off to sleep.

When I woke up, Sidney was there with a tray. He filled a mug from a pitcher of orange-brown foam.

"This is all the leftover vegetables and fruits, put through the juicer. Now, before you say anything, try it."

I sipped it cautiously. Sidney handed me a paper napkin holding a puffed rice cake.

"Don't *think* about eating it, or you'll think Styrofoam. Just tell yourself to insert wholesome substance into digestive system."

As I nibbled, the subtle flavor of toasted rice awakened a faint appetite. I drank more of the foamy juice. The weight of sickness began to lift.

"And now, nourishment for the soul," Sidney said. "I'm going to read you some Thomas Merton." He opened the book to a passage he had marked and read as if the words were coming from his own heart.

> *You flowers and trees, you hills and streams, you fields, flocks and wild birds, you books, you poems, and you people, I am unutterably alone in the midst of you . . . I try to touch you with the deep fire that is in the center of my heart, but I cannot touch you without defiling both you and myself, and I am abashed, solitary and helpless, surrounded by a beauty that can never belong to me.*

> *But this sadness generates within me an unspeakable reverence for the holiness of created things, for they are pure and perfect and they belong to God and they are mirrors of His beauty. He is mirrored in all things like sunlight in clear water: but if I try to drink the light that is in the water I only shatter the reflection. And so I live alone and chaste in the midst of the holy beauty of all created things, knowing that nothing I can see or hear or touch will ever belong to me.*

❖ ❖ ❖

That night I dreamed I was enlightened. My usual ment
activity fell away, receding like a wave on a beach, and then
there was nothing. For an instant, I knew: *this is it*. Then
another wave broke over me; my mind jabbered, my body fid-
geted, straining at being alive. Again the noise diminished,
the movement died, and there was nothing. So clear. So
empty. So nothing-special. Ah, yes, again: *this is it*. Another
wave crashing down, and with it the recognition that what
we consider normal functioning is a jumble of confusion and
striving and hyperactivity. Then again, nothing, nothingness,
utter freedom.

❖ ❖ ❖

The gong rang softly. Aromas wafting up from below carried
the good news that breakfast would be something other than
Joel's usual buckwheat groats. I had slept for most of the previous thirty-six hours, and I felt better. I showered and dressed
and went downstairs.

In the kitchen, Sidney was wearing the big white apron.
It looked miraculously fitting and fresh. He reminded me of the
Chinese bodhisattva Kwan Yin, embodying both masculine
strength and feminine softness, steadfast protection and incom-
parable sweetness, everything all at once.

Over omelettes and biscuits and strong tea, I told Sidney
my dream. He smiled and closed his eyes for a moment. Then
he told me a dream he had had once after staying up all night
reading a Tibetan Buddhist text.

"There was this special gathering, for those of us who have
been following the Buddha around all this time and still don't
get it. You know what I mean?"

I nodded.

"Plenty of us, right? Now, the Buddha himself was there. He sat down and invited us to come kneel beside him, one by one, so he could give each of us a special message. Long line of people. Great excitement all around. My friend Jack was right ahead of me. I watched him go and kneel, and the Buddha whispered into his ear. Then Jack got up. He's radiant, he's laughing in this weird way, and I realize, hey, old Jack looks *enlightened!* He's looking back at me with this incredibly compassionate smile. And I'm scared to death, because now it's my turn. I go and kneel, and the Buddha bends down to me and whispers the message."

Sidney lay his fork down, leaned close to my ear, and paused a moment. Then he whispered: "'Pretend enlightenment.'"

He slapped the table, laughing. "Funny thing is, it *works!* It's like your dream; you *were* enlightened at that moment. It's the same with pretending. You can say to yourself, how would it be this minute if I were enlightened? And how it would be is obvious—that knowledge is already in us. All that's required is a very subtle shift." He shook his head in amazement at his own realization.

Anna and Joel were gone, and Sidney and I spent the day at our separate tasks. I sorted mail, answered requests for information, then began processing registrations for upcoming retreats. The flu had left me below par, but seeing the stack of unprocessed forms get smaller and the completed stack bigger was sufficiently satisfying that I could ignore how weak I was.

After supper, Sidney and I went together to the meditation hall, walking silently up the stone steps, taking our shoes off at the door. Inside, I turned on a single low light, then realized that Sidney had not followed me in.

I took my cushion into the center of the room and settled into the stillness. I noticed that being tired made it easier to calm my mind. At normal levels of energy, my attention was captured by thought, and twenty minutes might pass before I remembered

I was on the cushion. But now thoughts seemed as weakened as my body, and they drifted away without gaining a foothold.

Through a window, a slow trace of movement tugged at my peripheral vision. Sidney, outside. The porch creaked with the regular give of floorboards. The unmistakable measured rhythm of walking meditation enveloped me in peace. A sensation of openness filled my chest, as if the whole region around my heart were exposed. I felt scared and at the same time safe, acutely alive.

My thoughts would wander, then a sound would draw my attention back to the present. Sitting still with a wild, full heart; not knowing what it meant. Wandering, buzzing thoughts. Then slipping back to the present. Sitting still with a wild longing. Wondering. Sitting. Just sitting. After an hour I left the meditation hall. I caught a glimpse of Sidney slowly, slowly turning a corner of the porch.

The next day, Sidney told me that in his walking meditation the night before, he had had the sense that when he turned the next corner, he would encounter his True Self. The expectation was so intense that as he neared the end of each wall, his heart knocked hard in his chest. His bare, aching yearning was almost palpable. I found myself wishing for his enlightenment, and, recalling my dream, even daring for an instant to hope for my own.

✧ ✧ ✧

In the kitchen, the answering machine flashed with a message. It was from Cheri, asking me to call her in California. I dialed the Zen Center number and left a message, and a little later, she called me back.

"Did I leave a blue bag there?" she asked. "It's my grandson's old diaper bag, and I carry my meditation bell in the side pocket. Would you look around for it?"

I picked up the big ballpoint pen Sidney had tied to the desk and scribbled a note to myself.

"I'll look," I said. "Listen, I'm glad you called. There's somebody here, and . . . I am sort of obsessed with him. . . ."

"Oh?"

I clicked the ballpoint tip in and out four or five times, then made myself stop. "We have been meditating together, and I don't know exactly what he has to do with it, but . . ." I wanted to put it in dharmic terms, but it came out sounding like a medical problem. "It feels as if my chest is wide open. Gaping. Like air is entering my thoracic cavity. A little scary."

She said it sounded like what people in her California group called the Big Feeling, and that sooner or later the Big Feeling is followed by a Big Opportunity. "It's important not to turn away from that. So when your heart is open, watch what causes it to close. Watch for the fear that will arise when you're in this unprotected state."

While she talked, I drew a meditation cushion on the notepad. I was only half listening, waiting for her to finish. What I wanted to say seemed more urgent, and I burst in as soon as she paused. "I've got this idea that Sidney is going to . . . to be important in my spiritual journey, and I'm wondering whether I should—"

"Remember," Cheri said, "between the 'should' and the 'should not' is an open space of possibility, where interesting things can happen. They may take unexpected forms, contrary to all rules. They may involve confusion and conflict. These are not reasons to avoid them. The only thing you want to avoid is turning away from your heart."

"How do you know what's your heart and what's ego?"

Same old answer: pay close attention. It takes practice. When you're suffering, take it as a sign that it's time to sit and meditate.

"It's just that I have this urge to . . . well, it's embarrassing, because I've never felt this toward you, but I want to sort of turn myself over to him. Spiritually, of course. Do you know what I mean?"

There was a pause before she answered. "I would examine this urge closely if I were you. Very, very closely. See if you can find out exactly what it is. Then see what's behind it, what's inside it, what's underneath it, what's beyond it."

"Are you talking about meditation?" I asked.

"I'm talking about on the cushion and off the cushion. Constant and compassionate attention."

A longer pause, then Cheri spoke again. "Now, each of us has her mindfulness issues to work on. Mine include keeping track of my belongings. Yours are to watch what happens to your heart and also to look for my bag."

That night, I lay awake for hours, exhausted but restless and unable to sleep. It was like a replay of the sleepless nights I'd spent during the work retreat, when I was obsessed by the "Popeye man." Now that he was a real person, I felt something of the same excitement, but I was scared too. It's one thing to deal with Desire completely within one's mind and within the strictures of a silent retreat, and quite another to have it complicated by actual presence of the Desired. The lust type of Desire was simple compared to what I felt now. It was as if all my feelings toward the swami in the ski cap, the Nashville Buddhist Temple, Achan Sobin, and the Popeye man before I knew him as Sidney got rolled up into a huge, hot, heavy, throbbing ball of pure longing. Through the hours of the night, the ball rolled back and forth across my mind. At one moment, that longing could be the most exquisite experience life has to offer, imbuing everything it touched with meaning. The next, it was a crushing burden, insupportable, the kind of difficulty that in the past had made me want to run away and start life over somewhere else.

The next day I made myself get up early, even though I had slept little and was still weak from having been ill. Trying not to think of how desperately I wanted to stay in bed, I spent the morning in the office, processing registration forms. As the sleep deficit hit me, though, seeing one pile of papers grow smaller and another grow larger lost its appeal. At some point, I put my head down on the desk, let my eyes close, and allowed myself to be taken over by sleep. Now and then, I would wake briefly, but I couldn't muster the strength to raise my head.

Once, slipping slowly upward from the depths of unconsciousness, I went through that strange little sequence that happens sometimes, when you first know simply that you exist, then recall where you are—oh, this room, I remember, and through the window those trees, yes—as if from a distant time and place. Finally, you remember *who* you are, and the last step is recalling what was going on in your life before you went to sleep. It all came back to me: Southern Dharma, Sidney, having the flu, Cheri asking me to watch—what was it I was supposed to watch? *Watch what happens to your heart.* I felt a million miles away from my heart. It was all too overwhelming, and I retreated once more into oblivion.

Some time later, into my sleep drifted the sounds of food being prepared in the kitchen. Gentle music: bowls and spoons, water running, knife zipping through vegetables and thumping on wood. Sidney's footfalls leaving the kitchen. Quiet.

Within the swelling silence, from its very heart, came the peal of the gong. I just let myself stay there, slumped onto the desk, allowing the vibrations to flow into the little room, into me, filling everything and passing through.

When Sidney came to the office door, I raised my head, and he gestured for me to follow him outside. The wooden cable spool that served as a picnic table was set with two places. From the kitchen, he brought out a platter of steamed vegetables, with a ruffle of fresh herbs around the edge and a bowl of dark, fragrant sauce in the middle. We sat quietly for a moment. The stillness was full of life: wasps nosing around the food, the two cats stalking each other in a patch of mint, treetops waving gently in the clear sky, midday sun falling like a blessing on the cove.

After we had eaten, Sidney asked if I would like to go up to the mountaintop and spend the whole night in meditation. "It's full moon," he said. "Asian Buddhists do all-night sittings every full moon. We could do walking meditation all the way up, sit at the top until dawn, and do walking meditation down again."

The prospect of a whole night without sleep was appalling. "Oh, no, I couldn't possibly," I moaned, sinking with disappointment.

"No problem," Sidney said, patting my arm. "Tell you what: I'll just show you my own style of walking meditation right here." He stood up.

"First, focus on something a few yards ahead of you, like that tree trunk, but maintain awareness of your entire field of vision. Without shifting your gaze, at the edge of your vision you can also see the herb garden and the woods. Now, keep focused on the tree and the peripheral awareness of the whole field. Take a step. The field of view changes. Take in the new field of view, keeping the awareness of the whole, then take another step. You regulate your speed so that your movement is not faster than your mind. Each step is . . . here . . . here . . . here. Thus. Thus. Thus. Where you are at a given moment—the thusness of it, rather than what you think about it—that's the bed of enlightenment."

It was as if he had peeled away the ideas and attitudes in which I had wrapped walking meditation—mainly that I should concentrate on doing it right—and handed me back the pure experience. For the first time, I saw walking meditation for itself, not just as a break from sitting but as a perfect opportunity for realizing oneness in each moment. I longed to try it out, right then and there, but I lacked the energy.

I was back in the office and Sidney was washing dishes when Joel came into the kitchen. I heard Sidney ask if he wanted to spend the night meditating on top of the mountain. Sure, Joel said; he could leave in an hour.

I tried to work but could not concentrate. My body pleaded exhaustion, but the thought of leaving the work unfinished was intolerable. So was the thought of having nothing special to claim me, while Joel and Sidney were off together, enjoying each other's company. I was tormented by envy. Then a little voice said, *When you're suffering, it's a sign that it's time to sit.*

I rose from the desk and walked to the meditation hall, propelled by what Cheri would call sheer willingness.

As I climbed the steps to the porch of the hall, I could see Sidney through the open door. He was standing behind the teacher's cushion at the front of the room, his back to me, arranging something on the narrow table. As I came closer, I saw that it was a large, flat stone, and on the stone was a clump of turf. Sidney turned it a little to one side, and a clod of dirt fell off. He picked it up, held it in his hand, squeezed it, and stuck it back on the big clump. He stepped back and looked, shifted the stone slightly, then turned, walked around the teacher's cushion, and sat down on his own cushion in the center of the room.

I entered the hall and looked at what Sidney had placed on the table. Damp clay sprouting bright new weeds from a carpet of pebbles and dead leaves and stalks, composting away, rich and ordinary and complete and perfect. The mirror of God, the earth itself, an altarpiece of unsurpassable beauty and expressiveness. The clump of earth acknowledged the mystery and miracle of all existence; the intricacy of even the smallest, most humble parts of it, which we ordinarily overlook; the richness and necessity of even those parts we condemn as low and dirty, from which we take pains to keep ourselves separate. Here—in the stone, the clay, the plant life—the connection was undeniable. From the dark, damp, sticky soil, the formless vessel of decay and disintegration, arise graceful stalks of the freshest green, and from the stalks sprout the tenderest leaves, and at the tips are tiny flower petals like specks of heaven in lavender and pale yellow and whitest white.

This was the offering I wanted to make, sophisticated and subtle, yet so simple, so sincere. This is the spirit I would have wanted to bring to my efforts at the Buddhist Temple. It was what I wished I had placed on this table long ago. *Why hadn't I?*

My heart clenched in rank envy. Sidney had made the most perfect offering. Not only was he kind and wise and caring and practically enlightened, he also had the gift of making the most telling, profound, magnificent gesture. He was, in fact, exactly what I longed to be, if only I were . . . what? Freer, clearer, more grounded, more present to myself. He is a true spiritual student, I thought. And I . . .

I went in and took my place on my cushion.

Sidney sat in perfect stillness. So did I.

After a while, Joel's footsteps approached along the path to the meditation hall, then paused. Sidney quietly got up and left.

Yearning roared within me. In desperate determination to find some way to stay put through my anguish, I envisioned Cheri before me on the teacher's cushion. I could see her there, unmoving, unmoved by my agitation. Her presence was a great comfort. My breathing calmed. The yearning rose again, and again. But as soon as I remembered, I could envision Cheri in front of me, sitting on her cushion in sublime ease.

What is this yearning? What is this reaction to Sidney? Where is the projection in this? I want to make the beautiful gesture. I want to *be* the beautiful gesture, front and center, seen and admired. I want to be good enough to . . . I could not say, could not think.

Sitting. Breathing.

. . . enough to deserve . . .

Breathing in. Breathing out.

The tiniest whisper of Cheri's voice: *To deserve your own True Self.* It was the merest trace of insight, here and then gone.

Gradually, some gentleness opened around my heart. Another rage of yearning, then back to the image of the teacher on the cushion, and again the gentleness, settling within me and around me.

I sat for a long time. All my tiredness was right there with me. Heavy limbs, heavy eyelids, heavy face, back hurting, the wish to lie down. But none of that seemed to require any action. Now and then, emotion rose in me, and I felt the desire to cry, but that too needed no action. I just sat. Heaviness, sadness, pain, and longing each had their place within a larger sense of ease, just letting it all be whatever it was. The cushion before me where I imagined Cheri sitting and my own cushion beneath me seemed held within the same soft space. No need to move at all, no need to do anything. Safe. Still. Spacious.

The spaciousness expanded to fill the room, and then beyond, out past the meditation hall, filling the cove and the valley and reaching up the mountain to embrace Joel and Sidney, as they made their silent way to the top.

✧ ✧ ✧

I got up after sleeping long and hard to find a note from Joel saying he would be away for the day. Sidney's bag of cat chow had disappeared from the kitchen. I went outside and looked through the trees to the parking lot. His truck was gone.

How could he leave and not tell me? There was so much I wanted from him, and there hadn't been enough time. . . .

The pang of abandonment was like a bell reminding me: *suffering is a sign to sit*. Without stopping to eat breakfast, I followed the gravel path and then the stone steps to the meditation hall. Up the porch steps, shoes off, in the door, bowing, walking to the cushion in the middle of the room, bowing, taking my seat, bowing. Sitting.

The table in the front of the room was bare. Stone slab gone, clump of turf gone.

Teacher's cushion empty.

Watching my heart open and close, watching longing arise within the sweet, aching vulnerability.

❖ ❖ ❖

I was eating leftovers at the kitchen counter when the telephone rang.

Cheri, cheerful. "Guess what I found? My blue bag. So. How are you doing?"

"Was I euphoric when we talked yesterday? Or was that even yesterday?" I heard myself sigh. She rejoices in my suffering, I thought. I bet she's thinking, *now* we have something to work with.

"Something's changed?" Cheri asked.

"Everybody's gone."

"Maybe it's a good time to be alone. You can just be with you."

"Well, actually, I sort of know that. I've been feeling this intense yearning, and something tells me it's better to work through this by myself. But I can't help but feel that Sidney— I guess he embodies everything I want in my life."

"Like what?"

"Oh—beauty. And commitment to meditation. And being taken care of."

"He's everything you fail to recognize in yourself."

"What do you mean?"

"Beauty is already there. It's an experience. But you can't experience beauty while you're thinking about how you don't have beauty in your life. All you have to do to experience beauty is to get out of the way. Everything is already available, right here."

"But being taken care of requires somebody else."

"Does it?"

"Well, doesn't it?"

"You can take care of yourself. Is there some way you're not doing that?"

She sounded like a father, mother, nanny, and therapist rolled into one, but even within my resistance, part of me heard what she was saying. I thought about how tired I had been while working away at the desk.

"Watch for the point at which you become unlovable to yourself," Cheri said. "Then be very, very kind. This is where the practice of compassion begins. You may encounter lots of things that try to pull you off in other directions, but the thing to remember is, don't turn away from your heart. See if you can stay with yourself, being completely present. The way you would with someone you love."

"You know, in a funny way I feel almost elated, but at the same time, I'm exhausted. I feel at the edge of something— almost like despair."

"My advice is, plunge into it. And don't forget to keep looking. Stay with it. Just like sitting."

"All right," I said. "I'm going to do that. I'll be the big doll and watch the stories that get played out. I'll see everything I can. And I'll report back to you."

We said good-bye, and I climbed to the loft. The bed I had made under the skylight, the lamp and stack of books and magazines beside it, and the comfortable nest I had constructed with such happy anticipation no longer signified rest and release, or anything at all. I was absorbed in my determination to keep looking, to "see."

Kneeling on the bed, I envisioned myself as a Zen warrior, ready for anything. I waited. All that happened was the drearily familiar urge to curl up and cry.

I am trying to *see what is*, I reminded myself, however ignoble. I am looking for the awful truth.

I curled up and cried.

Ask yourself who is feeling this, I heard Cheri's voice say. *What does that person look like?*

In my mind, there appeared a lumpen form, hunched at a desk, moving papers around and writing on them and clipping things together and stacking them up in a big rush, as if getting the job finished quickly were a matter of life-and-death urgency.

Ask whatever you want to know, Cheri often said.

"What's the rush?" I silently asked.

The figure replied clearly, "To hold off disaster."

"What disaster?"

The figure crumbled to nothing, and the answer to my question appeared in a second figure: a hard-edged image of a woman in motorcycle regalia, tight black leather with silver studs, glossy black boots. All the surfaces of her body and clothes were unnaturally smooth, taut, as if tooled by machine, and she exuded a powerful perfection. For a moment, I wondered: might this idealized image represent if not my True Self, at least some better, stronger self?

Keep asking, Cheri says, *and believe nothing*.

I didn't know what to say. I was very uncomfortable, part of me cringing with embarrassment and feeling foolish. But I kept still and silent, my attention on the image. It took on a mechanical quality, which became increasingly sinister. Suddenly, anxiety coursed through me like an electric shock. The words WORK-NAZI flashed above the image.

"What do you want?" I asked tentatively.

Again, the reply was clear. The Work-Nazi wanted the first figure, the office worker, done away with. The Work-Nazi's aim is to obliterate any who are weak, who contradict the image of invincibility and energetic purposefulness. Her message was, deviation from the ideal cannot be tolerated; ordinary human frailty is despised.

Believe nothing.

At the first hint that the Work-Nazi's standards might be questioned, fine cracks appeared in her figure. The more confident my questioning, the more the cracks widened. I saw that inside the figure was something hideous, rotten, repugnant. That something was so shameful, so threatening that it had to be concealed beneath a constant projection of the opposite qualities: strength, hardness, smoothness, invincibility. "What is so threatening?" I asked.

The cracked shell of the Work-Nazi fell away to reveal a pale, thin, misshapen child, lying naked and grimy on a shabby cot. The child is everything the Work-Nazi fears: helpless, flawed, pathetically vulnerable. Horrified that this figure represented some aspect of me, I almost turned away. But something held me there. Just looking, seeing what is.

Suddenly, the nature of suffering seemed so obvious, and so sad. How hard we try to insulate ourselves from threats that are purely imaginary, one part of the personality covering up the vulnerability of another, layer upon layer. I sobbed, stricken at the uselessness, the wasted effort of maintaining these manifold false identities. All of us, pretending, trying to protect . . . what? The semblance of invulnerability, of being in control. Our absurd need to be other than human.

When the tears subsided, I got back onto my knees. I want to see more, I said to myself. I want to see as much as I can.

What exactly is happening right now?

Pressure in my chest, which I interpret as an emotional ache.

What emotion?

Hm, sort of generic. Instant vignettes demonstrated that I could have whatever story I wished: I am alone here, left out; I will never learn meditation; I should go somewhere else, try something else. After following a few of the familiar story lines, I began to lose track, and it became impossible to take any of them very seriously.

But, wait, I am having this big experience, I said to myself . . . now, let's see, what was it? I would almost give in to a smile, then the old hard habit would reassert itself: to sink into feeling awful, to abandon hope, to abdicate responsibility, to see myself as beyond redemption.

This is where the practice of compassion begins: with whatever exists in yourself that you cannot love.

Little by little, there appeared the possibility of not indulging in the drama of feeling awful.

The willingness to look rather than to turn away is in itself acceptance, I remembered Cheri saying. *And in acceptance is compassion.*

Finally, I lay down.

Whatever it was I longed for, I was not going to get it from Sidney, or Cheri, or anybody. The world wrapped me in aloneness—and everyone else, too.

Through the skylight, I watched the long rectangle of sky blanche with the midday sun. Then I closed my eyes. The only movement in my body was my breath, so light I could hardly feel it.

It was dark when I awoke. I switched on the lamp. Its warm circle of light fell around me. Reflected in the skylight above, I could see a fold of plaid blanket, a white square of pillow, and on it the dark head of a familiar stranger—myself, as I had not seen myself before. I stared, mesmerized, as the narrow bed took on the semblance of an ambulance stretcher, and I became a witness to my own woundedness and vulnerability.

After a while, I was simply seeing my reflection again, and it seemed all right to be lying down, doing nothing; it seemed natural to be tired. The aerial view gave me some distance, and I kept looking, looking at the one from whom I had so often turned away. I was getting to know her.

Terribly, terribly tired. All right to go back to sleep again. I switched off the lamp, and through the window glimpsed the moon, high and bright.

I awoke in the morning to a sensation of extraordinary softness, my body feeling like a cloud, almost not there. The window showed pink-gray dawn and the faint reflection of the same dark head on the pillow. I was with myself, looking into the mirror of the world.

CHAPTER 14

DHARMA, KARMA, AND LETTING GO

CAN OTHERS AID US ON OUR JOURNEY?
A PARADOX, RESOLVED IN GRATITUDE.

When I got back home, I called Cheri to say I had been through the emotional equivalent of open-heart surgery and survived. It had felt as if a hollowness gaped in my chest, as if my breath flowed back and forth through a boundless empty space in the region I call my heart. Eventually, the sensation had waned, but Cheri said not to worry that the loss was permanent. Having had the experience of turning to sitting, to myself—she called it "turning the stream of compassion inward"—I could always remember it, refer back to it, know that it was possible, and if I kept practicing, my heart would open again and again.

I know no more now than I did then about bodhisattvas, or about enlightenment. I have no answer to the koan, "Who are the sentient beings we vow to save?" I am less certain about what anybody can do to aid anybody else's spiritual journey. Causality, like identity, is one of those things that seems to shift, become elusive, in a certain phase of this path. I am thinking of the saying, "Before Zen practice, a mountain is just a mountain; during Zen practice, a mountain is not a mountain; after Zen practice, a mountain is just a mountain again." The middle part of that saying suggests to me the way in which this practice calls into question our most solid assumptions. One of those for me has always been that people can be of help to one another.

Now something less definite, less solid seems to be the case: that certain people present us with situations we can use to grow. Such situations may offer us anything from information to insight, from supportive encouragement to aggressive challenge. Another person's mere presence may affect one's life in profound ways that cannot be precisely defined.

Looking back at how others seem to have guided and eased my journey, those who were the most helpful were not (as far as I know) attempting to do anything *for* me. They were simply following their own paths. Sidney and I crossed paths at a time when I was ready to ready to receive what he had to give. He demonstrated for me not only the commitment one might bring to meditation practice but also the passion. He made things I had scarcely hoped for seem real, reachable, of ultimate importance, and yet he brought to all that a lightness of spirit that in itself was a teaching. He opened a door for me.

I can even sometimes imagine that Jane, who broke my heart, also opened a door, but because I was unable or unwilling to turn and head in that direction, she gave me a shove. Not an altruistic shove, but still a compassionate one, if only in the compassion she showed herself in getting out of a situation she could not handle.

Cheri insists not only that I walk through each door on my own but also that I *notice* that I do so. When I speak of her skill as a teacher and try to thank her, her firm rejoinder is always the same: "There are no good teachers, only good students." I never know how to respond to that. Actually, I don't believe it. I think there is such a thing as an exceptionally gifted teacher. On the other hand, the gratitude I feel is not so much for something she or anyone else does as it is for their very being. Understanding that enables me to focus my effort on my own path, my own being, in the faith that that is how I will most benefit others. Indeed, the concept of "other"—defining what I am not—may slip into unimportance.

Sidney and I became long-distance dharma friends. When I told him about the various emotional reactions I had had toward him, he laughed his big-hearted laugh. Recognizing one's projections, he said, is an important step toward deeper awareness.

Before long, I saw the difficult areas in Sidney's life—dark moods, erratic employment, a compulsiveness in his need to help others, which often overrode common sense. He also suffered from a chronic illness for which the medication itself was a problem. If he took enough drugs to alleviate his symptoms, he couldn't sleep, which was one reason he spent whole nights in meditation.

Sidney evolved from being a spiritual hero on a pedestal to someone whose struggles were humanly heroic. As we got to know each other better, we practiced maintaining a steady attentiveness in our communication with each other, rather than slipping off into various illusions offered by ego. Often we failed, but—just as in meditation—we tried again. Eventually, we were able to see and accept each other's fears and foolishness and longing and confusion and recognize the same in ourselves. In him, I began to see my own moods, my darkness, my unsettledness, my delusions. What really surprised me was discovering in myself the admirable and attractive qualities I had attributed to Sidney: generosity, lightheartedness, a love of beauty, and even a commitment to spiritual practice. Those were the hardest to admit to. When Sidney and I were deep in the process of letting go of preconceptions and looking ever more clearly, seeing not only ourselves but all people, all beings, there were moments that took my breath away.

As it turned out, Sidney was the one to realize my fantasy of spending time at the Buddhist Temple. I told him they needed his skills; I told Min about him, and the two of them came up with a plan for Sidney to work on the building in exchange for food and lodging.

Sidney's example, however, was not enough to make me meditate regularly. When I did sit, sometimes my attention became fixed so firmly on anything other than the present that I would find myself standing and looking out the window or in another room or changing clothes before realizing that I had left the cushion. I told Cheri about it, and sometimes she made a suggestion, such as sitting more often for shorter periods, but mostly she repeated her old favorite lines. *Whatever you do, pay attention to it. Embrace it all in compassion. Keep coming back to the breath, to body sensations, to the present moment.*

❖   ❖   ❖

That fall, Cheri invited me to join her for the week of workshops at the rafting center near Southern Dharma. The people who had been to her retreat and the previous workshop were eager for more. Others were wary about Buddhism but interested in meditation. Some simply wanted to hear Cheri talk or to meet with her for guidance. For me, it was a chance to do an individual semiretreat, with plenty of time outdoors in a beautiful setting.

The long drive to North Carolina gave me time to play out in my mind all the possibilities lurking within the idea of traveling with the teacher. These ranged from spontaneous enlightenment to vaguely imagined disasters (indeed, from the ego's point of view, enlightenment—loss of ego—*would* be a disaster). Might Cheri discover how deeply flawed I was and abandon me? And what about the people at the rafting center? In their eyes, I imagined, I might be the opposite, a chosen one, a one-person entourage, the austere Zen counterpart of the rapt disciples who trail Indian gurus. That was not a role I relished: there would be too many expectations that I would be unable to meet. Could spiritual teachers have regular friendships? I wondered. If so, did that imply that I was now a friend, that Cheri had given up on me as a student? Or could it be that I had demonstrated such subtle but profound progress off the cushion that I was the only person in the world who did not need to meditate? Was I in some special category I did not know about? Egocentricity churned away in the desperate need to know, Who Am I?

At the airport, Cheri stopped on our way out to make a telephone call. I carried her larger bag to the car, then drove around to pick her up. She was carrying the blue diaper bag, which she put on the floorboard between her feet and the gearshift. Tucked into the outside pocket of the bag were two books. The inscrutable eye of Rajneesh stared me down from one, while the wretched excess of Arnold Schwarzenegger decorated the other.

"Rajneesh again!" I fumed. "You must know about all those Rolls Royces. . . ."

"I've heard he doesn't actually drive them," Cheri said. "They just sit there, I'm told. In a long line. Quite a comment, wouldn't you say?"

On what? I wondered. Consumer culture? No, she must mean something more Buddhist. Desire, maybe: its ubiquity, its insatiability. But Cheri was going on about how Rajneesh's cars, whether he drives them or not, might be useful in breaking down illusions of purity and piety and the like, which are misleading about the teacher's true role.

"Which is what?" I asked.

The teacher's life is not a set of rules for other people to emulate, Cheri said. The role of the teacher is to be a mirror, to assist students in seeing themselves, in recognizing their attachments and letting go, in waking up to their true nature. Rajneesh, she had heard, was very skillful at that. I recalled Achan Sobin saying that he would like to teach behind a mirror, so that when students looked toward him, they would see only themselves.

"Since my own car karma seems to run to secondhand vans," Cheri went on, "and I'm not all that attracted by tobacco or alcohol or any of the other levelers, shall we say, of teachers' reputations, I figure diet cola will have to do."

Reputation. The word lodged in my mind. And *reputedly* suggests that something is not necessarily so, which points up the flimsy nature of "reputation." And what is the relevance of reputation if the teacher merely reflects back what is in the student? I thought of Achan's laughing about U Pandita and American women and how for a moment I had fully believed to be true something that I had imagined—that Achan was concerned about U Pandita's reputation—and how Achan's own reputation in my eyes was briefly tarnished when I judged his attitude to the whole subject as inappropriate.

It was too much to think about, and I shifted to a topic on which my opinions were firm: I wanted Cheri to stop drinking diet cola. I had considered sending her copies of research reports on the health hazards of artificial sweetener, I told her, with a note attached quoting her own comment that nobody in their right mind would drink poison.

"Did I say that?" she asked with a grin.

"You did. Although," I assured her quickly, "I've realized that trying to catch the teacher in contradictions doesn't get me anywhere."

"Well, it's so easy, there's no sport in it!" she replied. "But it's an interesting thing to look at. What's the intention behind watching for contradictions in someone else? Why would one latch onto a teacher's errors, except as a reason to dismiss the teaching? And what, other than ego, would have any investment in that?"

Well, yes, that was an interesting point, I had to admit.

"But you can rest your mind about poisons," she said, "because I've quit drinking diet cola."

"Oh—really?"

"Pretty much."

"Well, that kind of lets the air out of my balloon."

"That's what I do all day, you know. People come in with these balloons of greed, hatred, and delusion—or passion, aggression, and ignorance, depending on which Buddhists you listen to—and my job is to let the air out," she said. "Sometimes gently, sometimes with a bang."

My mind was a jumble of thoughts and feelings: the need to watch signs so I would get onto the right highway, a desire to make the best use of the time by asking for spiritual guidance, apprehension about my balloons being popped. Once we got onto the interstate, I went for the guidance, launching into a well-rehearsed account of current sources of suffering in my life.

I was haunted by Roy. Had my behavior had anything to do with his abrupt departure from Southern Dharma? Had he been hurt or angry or confused by my on-and-off gestures of friendship? If I had really paid attention to him, if I had been able to find some oneness between us, might he have stayed on there, to be healed and redeemed and transformed into a worthy citizen? And my intense reaction to Sidney had forced me to face aspects of myself I was loath to acknowledge: the expectation that someone take care of me, and when attention was withdrawn, feeling unbearably bereft and seeing myself as diminished, insufficient. At times, I was still overcome with the same undefined longing I had felt then.

And, of course, there was Jane. Whenever I felt low about other relationships, or about anything at all, the whole trauma of being "kicked out of therapy," as I thought of it, arose yet again in all its ghastliness. In fact, I had once again brought along The Letter. Of course, I couldn't read it to Cheri while I was driving, and asking her to reach into the back and rummage through my bag to find it . . . no, no, no. Focus on the positive, I told myself.

I told Cheri about an idea that had come to me for dealing with all those troubling issues: somehow I should transcend my personality and the social realm, turn away from people and their opinions, and look inward to myself. Cheri's response so startled me that I was left speechless. Her suggestion was the opposite: that I focus on deepening my relationships. I could think of each person, she said, as being in my life for some karmic purpose, and so to withdraw might not be helpful. Seeing that I was about to query her again on the subject of karma, she said that understanding karma was not the point.

"The point is not to be afraid to take risks with other people," she said. "Not to think you have to be a certain way to be loved. And while you're at it, not to expect yourself to be a model of equanimity when something affects you strongly."

"Well, the funny thing is, sometimes everything is fine, and I am all equanimity. But then I start thinking," I said dolefully, "and I am taken over by the same feelings all over again."

"Oh, yes, indeed, these conditioned responses tend to come up again and again and again, for a very long time. I call conditioning the 'viscous cycle' because it's such sticky stuff."

"It sure is. I've tried everything—"

"Except letting go, right?" Cheri interjected. "My recommendation is to stop struggling to figure out anything about anybody else. It's what you're feeling about yourself that causes anger or resentment or despair, not what someone else does. Can you see that? Shall we explore it a little right now?"

"Ah . . . I guess . . . yes. I'm willing to try."

"Okay, now, think of Roy or Sidney or Jane, and let's go back to my favorite question. Can you see what in you is like them?"

For an instant, I felt defensive. Then, for another instant, my mind went blank. The realization that followed was sudden and clear and painful: how often I had done the rejecting.

"I see." My words were a strangled croak. "All the times I've walked away. And not even said why."

"Do you know why?"

I cleared my throat, recovered my voice, sighed, and heard myself say, "I got in too deep and just wanted out. I was desperate."

"What's behind 'wanting out'?" Cheri asked.

I waited to see what it was. "Fear," I said.

"Of what?"

Nothing more came to me. We rode in silence.

After a while, Cheri spoke. "Isn't it possible that Jane acted out of the same feelings that motivated you in those situations?"

That Jane might act from weakness or fear or confusion, that she and I might somehow be on a par, had never occurred to me. I said nothing.

"Of course, we *do not know*," Cheri said. "Maybe it was something very simple. Maybe she decided you were just fine as you were, so there was nothing to fix. That's my own projection, of course. But it's a good thing to consider. Maybe there really *is* nothing wrong—with you or with her. Anyway, it isn't necessary for us to figure out what Jane thought. What we do know is that you made a shift from therapy to spiritual practice, and that seems to have been . . . a good move. Wouldn't you say?"

I agreed. Also, maybe I had to get beyond idealizing a person I considered wise and good and caring before I could work effectively with a spiritual teacher. Maybe that had something to do with why I was on this trip with Cheri. Maybe not. In any case, here we were, riding along together.

I asked Cheri something else I had been wondering about. Why had she never criticized what I saw as my lack of discipline in sitting meditation?

"You'll do it when you're ready," she said. "There's no point in using meditation as a way to make yourself feel guilty. One day you'll get so curious about how all this works, you'll sit down and start watching. You already see subpersonalities, which is a lot more of your own mind than you knew was there. Not that everybody accesses the information in the same way. The subpersonality route may suit you and not the next person. Eventually, you can know your own experience directly, in your body. But wherever your focus is, if you look, you'll see more. Projection, conditioning . . ."

"It sounds more psychological than spiritual," I observed.

She paused for a moment. "I hardly ever recommend that people read about Buddhism, because they tend to do that instead of meditating. But you might take a look at some of the original Buddhist texts. What little I've read in them sounds pretty psychological to me. It's amazing to find all these things we experience today right there in teachings from twenty-five hundred years ago."

✧ ✧ ✧

Dusk fell quickly as we headed down through a gorge to the river. Above the dark rim of mountains, the sky held a trace of sunset, faint wings of beige cloud across deep blue. At the rafting center, we went into the restaurant to get directions to the cabin where we would be staying. Cheri bought a diet cola from a machine. "No reason to be rigid about these things," she said, as she opened the can. I watched her drinking it in a telephone booth, where she made another call.

By the time we got to the cabin, it was very dark. The gravel road ended at the edge of a small field. Loaded with bags, we stepped gingerly through deep, damp grass. Cheri left her shoes outside the door, suggesting that I do the same. She accepted my offer to sleep in the living room and let her have the bedroom; she liked privacy, she said. I arranged my sleeping bag on the couch and unpacked, and when Cheri came out, we fixed cups of tea. Then we went out onto the tiny porch, which was nearly filled by a wooden swing, and sat in the dark.

After a while, Cheri spoke. "Could I ask you something? Don't feel obliged to tell me if you don't want to."

For once, she seemed uncertain, searching for words. "I'm not entirely clear about the nature of your attraction to Sidney," she began.

"Well, me either. Except it wasn't just . . . 'lust.' Which I've been duly warned about by a Buddhist monk."

"What was it?"

The most obvious answer, as she had pointed out, was that I saw in Sidney many things I wanted for myself and believed I lacked. But beyond that was a simpler truth: I just longed to be close to somebody. To feel loved. Lust seemed like one relatively small aspect of a much larger picture. When I really paid attention to the physical sensations in what I called "longing," they arose from a tenderness of heart that sometimes spilled over and flooded my whole body.

Cheri nodded. "Nothing wrong with love, you know. Nothing wrong with lust, either, but it's good to be clear about what the feeling is. There's nothing wrong with wanting. This is a common misconception about Buddhism. The only problem is being attached to the outcome. That's what causes suffering. There's no reason not to have what you want. From a spiritual point of view, it doesn't matter whether you get what you want or not. Putting an end to suffering has nothing to do with that. So while you're learning how to end suffering, you might as well go ahead and try to get what you want—remembering, of course, to pay close attention to everything that happens. Allowing yourself to have what you want, in the short run, is a way of being kind to yourself. That's my approach, anyway. I don't see how you can go wrong if you follow your heart, wherever it takes you."

I wondered what she had intended in starting the conversation, but I got so caught up in my own thoughts about it that I didn't ask. And maybe I didn't want to know.

✧ ✧ ✧

Each morning before breakfast, Cheri led a short sitting meditation. Most of the people who showed up were those who had been to Southern Dharma. Each evening she gave a workshop, which consisted of an hour or two of questions and answers, awareness exercises, and discussion. Several times as many people came to the workshops as to meditation, and more appeared each evening.

During the day, Cheri met with people individually. Careful not to infringe on her limited free time, I made myself scarce, taking walks and sitting in the restaurant overlooking the river, thinking about things she had said.

Cheri always turned me back to myself, firmly asserting that I alone was responsible for my practice, my experience, my life. Of course, there is no meaningful alternative to accepting that responsibility. And yet resistance arises in infinite variety: I cannot do these things for these reasons, I am too occupied with these other things to take on anything else, I never asked for this experience, other people don't have to put up with this, I can't help it, I have bad luck. . . . Everybody's excuses basically come down to the same process: resistance to what is.

In the workshop discussions, I had noticed also how the strong feelings that arise in people inevitably boil down to the same thing: fear of not having what one needs and the struggle to protect oneself against vulnerability. In everyone's efforts to make things better, in everyone's assumption that something was wrong, I saw the root of my own anguish, and it looked the same as theirs.

"Never assume inadequacy," Cheri admonished us one night. She offered a visualization of the alternative: the absolute adequacy of everything. "See if you can come with me in this," she said. "I imagine my body as a stalk, and at the top of the stalk, the universe opens out, extending from my sense organs in all directions, infinitely. That's my entire world, that's me. I am the whole thing. There is no separation. There's just everything that is. Now, what are the implications of experiencing ourselves this way?"

Raul spoke. "Everything is already mine, it's all right there, so I don't need anything. And if it's all mine, I want to treat it carefully, to be gentle and kind, not to do anything destructive."

"Yes," Cheri whispered. "Exactly. Other people are beings in your reality whom you do well to treat with respect and compassion. They are you yourself. They may nevertheless surprise you and cause difficulty, which you can meet responsibly, accepting that this is all yours, even though you are not in control of it."

So that was what she meant about taking responsibility for oneself and for the whole world: they are the same thing.

The next day, I put the letter from Jane in my pocket and went to a footbridge over the river. I had intended to read it one last time, as a sort of farewell ritual, and then to tear it into bits, but I didn't. I didn't even think about what it said. I just dropped it into the whitewater below, where it instantly disappeared.

CHAPTER 15

A YELLOW LIFE JACKET

NO ROLES. NO RULES.

With early-morning meditation, back-to-back appointments all day, and workshops each night, Cheri had almost no time to herself. I saw her in the telephone booth at the restaurant now and then and wondered to whom she was talking. Sometimes I heard her in the morning—she had borrowed some hand weights and spent half an hour doing a Schwarzenegger workout—but usually she left the cabin before I woke up and was at meditation when I arrived. Sometimes we saw each other for a few minutes late at night, and once, when someone cancelled a guidance appointment, she came in and energetically swept the cabin. A certain amount of dirt and vegetation attached itself to shoes coming through the deep grass outside, and some of it made its way into the living room. Cheri pointed that out to me, reminding me again to leave my shoes at the door.

Her nonstop pace worried me, but she said she was planning an afternoon off for a kayaking lesson with Raul. One day toward the end of the week, I noticed that she looked pale. I wondered if she could be tiring out. Tiredness being something I was ashamed to acknowledge in myself, I pushed the thought aside.

When I saw her next, that night back at the cabin, she was flushed with anger. I felt it as soon as I opened the door, a hot wave of fury just ahead of the verbal blast. On the table between us, like an accusation, lay a bright yellow life jacket. Cheri had needed a ride, or the keys to my car, to go upriver for the kayaking lesson. She had been counting on me, and I was nowhere to be found—"unavailable," as she put it. She had spent her one free afternoon waiting for me. On top of it all, I kept tracking dirt into the cabin.

I made a weak attempt to explain my side, but Cheri was not finished. As she raved, I had moments of seeing clearly that the anger was hers, not caused by me. Then she flung the life jacket onto the couch, stormed into the bedroom, and slammed the door.

Pushing the life jacket to the floor, I crumpled onto the couch, almost moaning in misery, but not daring to make a sound. I burrowed into my sleeping bag and began constructing my defense. She hadn't *told* me she needed the ride. So how could it be my fault? I ran through the obvious I'm-right, you're-wrong tapes from my internal collection—the standard repertoire, ready to be played at any moment—and I cranked out a few more strident (if no less clichéd) numbers, like "You think you're so sensitive, but you're actually completely self-ish" and "How can you do this to me?" But even as I was thinking the words, I saw the process as generic self-defense, the automatic response of ego, having nothing to do with this particular situation.

How to take responsibility in this? I wondered.

First, ask, *What is going on right now?*

I am shaken because Cheri lost her temper. *And?* I am afraid she doesn't like me.

But that's not what she said, I told myself.

Defensiveness rose again, and, again, protecting myself through explanation or apology or counterattack seemed beside the point. So she was angry. That did not require guilt or penance or, indeed, any action on my part.

The bedroom door opened. Cheri looked me in the eye and spoke calmly.

"We are here together, Sara, but you behave as if you're alone. Are you willing to look at how you do that?"

The door closed.

We are together here, and you act as if you are alone. Look at how you do that.

Scenes arose in my mind from throughout my life: how, so often, I had "acted as if I were alone." All my running from this thing to that, as if unconnected to anything or anyone. My intense pursuit of work, my headlong rush into whatever captured my fantasy, without regard for consequences to others— without awareness of others, really. Tracking dirt inside was a small manifestation of the same attitude.

Then a previously unthinkable idea passed through: was it possible that Cheri wanted to feel more connected with me? That my actions might affect her as they did others? That she might feel even some small degree of the hurt I myself felt at being forgotten, ignored, dismissed by Jane?

Look at how, when we are here together, you act as if you are alone. I pulled my head inside the sleeping bag, wracked with the agony of separateness.

Through the relatively minor miscommunication about the car keys and the kayaking lesson, Cheri somehow had touched on a pattern in my psyche, which, now that it was pointed out to me, I clearly recognized. Yes, I could see that, unconsciously, I behaved toward other people as if we were not connected. Truth opened like a door: it was so clear how, out of unacknowledged fear, I kept my distance. With Roy, it was out of fear of some unspeakable worst in myself, and the distancing was overt. With Sidney, it was more subtle: fear of something better than I dared imagine for myself spurred me to project all goodness onto him, as I had with Jane. With everyone I had ever been close to, I would find some way to withdraw, to justify being separate.

I kept watching, steadily watching, until I could face without flinching my suffering and my attempts to hide it. What had been agony gradually became merely *what is*. A clear, alert curiosity arose in me. Again, I wondered, could Cheri think I didn't want to be with her? Might she feel ordinary human vulnerability?

Then it was as if my suffering recognized the possibility of suffering in her, as if my pain bowed to her pain. The hurt I feel when someone turns away from me is no different from the hurt I cause in others. Our fears are the same, our blind spots, our courage, and our equivocating efforts at loving, all the same, all of us. As Joel had said, we are in the same boat on the sea of suffering. *Seeing connection instead of difference and separateness, feeling my pain as yours, yours as mine, one pain, we fall into the heart of compassion.*

The space opened again in my chest. It felt like sadness at the inevitability of misunderstanding and loss, and the impossibility of guarding against it. But I also felt freedom, like a cool breeze, in the wake of loosening my grip on the belief that I could or should protect myself from pain.

Then, the nameless yearning arose, more intensely than ever.

I imagined what Cheri would say. *You cannot make things happen, but you can let go of the belief that you must have something or that you cannot have it. You can simply be open and embrace what is longed for when it comes, in whatever form it takes. Look closely at the experience of longing—and the assumption that you must do something about it.*

But what is the longing?

The longing is always for one's True Self.

The next morning I woke up early, wondering how I would make amends to Cheri—not that I had done something wrong, but I wanted to show that I understood and cared about her feelings. I tapped softly on her door, but there was no answer. I was both disappointed and relieved that she had already gone.

As I left the cabin, I noticed the life jacket next to the door. I put it on; somehow it just seemed the right thing to do. When I entered the room where we met for meditation, I knew that the life jacket communicated all that needed to be said. *Look at me. I'm taking responsibility for my own salvation.*

I couldn't help smiling as I bowed and took my seat in the circle of cushions. Cheri bowed and smiled back. No need to rehash, explain, defend, protect, go back to what had been or forward to fear of what might be. Here we are, now, together, and that's enough.

✧ ✧ ✧

By afternoon, it was no longer quite enough. I wanted to find some way to express my gratitude. The trail where I walked was lined with the lavender asters that grace the woods in the early fall. I was aware of a local taboo against picking wildflowers, but the feathery arcs of tiny pale stars were irresistible, and I decided that any guilt involved would be worth it. I broke off several of the most perfect sprays and took them back to the cabin, where I arranged them in a tall glass on the kitchen table. I thought of putting them in Cheri's room so she would know they were for her. But even though her door was slightly ajar, I decided against going in.

When we arrived for the evening workshop, something felt wrong. One by one, we crept to our seats and sat perfectly still. I sensed a pall of intimidation, as if we were third-graders whose teacher was about to announce some punishment for our misbehavior.

A long and terrible silence was finally broken by Cheri's whisper.

"Here is a little koan for you." Cheri did not move, did not lift her gaze. "Let me remind you that a koan is a sort of Zen riddle, designed to jolt the mind out of its usual patterns."

The very space of the room seemed rigid with apprehension.

Cheri spoke softly. "I am an intensely private person. This afternoon when I went back to my cabin, someone had been in my room. My reaction was to feel violated. This whole place suddenly changed from wonderful to threatening. So I sat in meditation, I allowed all that to arise, and I watched my reactions. And I said to myself, 'Spiritual practice really does work, because before I started meditating, I might have been completely undone by this.'

"Whoever came into my room did so to leave me a present. Almost everyone in the world would agree that to leave a present in another person's room is a nice thing to do. But I experienced it very differently."

I was acutely perplexed. What exactly was she talking about?

Cheri raised her eyes and looked around at us.

"You may be thinking that I shouldn't have such an extreme reaction to someone coming into my room," she said. "I've thought that myself, many times. Why should I feel invaded? Why can't I sleep unless the door is closed? Why don't I just sleep out in the open? If I were really doing spiritual practice right, wouldn't I be perfectly at home anywhere? No boundaries, no conflicts, no fears, no anything? Now, this koan is not for you to answer, but to ponder."

After another long silence, a man raised his hand. Cheri nodded to him. He stammered out his question, attempting, it seemed, to speak the confusion we all felt.

"I don't understand, about sleeping in the open. Why would you . . . ?"

"Ah," Cheri said. "I see you don't have this particular preconceived idea about holy persons. Truly holy persons, many people believe, don't have possessions and don't have their own rooms. They just stretch out wherever they are. On a bed of nails, maybe. In a hair shirt. And then they don't sleep, and when they get up, they don't eat. Isn't that a common idea of holy people? What kind of a spiritual person am I if I sleep in a room with a door? And keep it closed? And don't want people to come in?"

No one moved or made a sound. Then a woman said, "So you do have an ego?"

Cheri responded firmly. "This is where it's helpful to remember about projection. You can know that that's true of *you*, that you have an ego. And remember, too, that egocentricity is the same as being identified with the illusion of separateness. And to the degree that we believe that illusion, we suffer.

"Now, this koan is whatever puzzles you about what has happened here tonight. It's important to be aware that the 'answer' to a koan does not lie in the plane of our ordinary thinking. The point is this: it is dangerous to assume we know anything. Assuming that we know something keeps us from being present to what is here in the moment. When we're lost in our idea of what is so, it never occurs to us that we need to drop that idea and come back to the present.

"That's a lot to try to grasp, I know. So if you are not seeing this clearly, don't worry. Most of us continue to struggle with it. We may have an intellectual understanding, but what we're aiming for in this practice is moment-by-moment awareness. Am I identified with that illusion of separateness right now? Is it possible to drop that and simply come back to the moment, come back to the breath? If I just bring the attention back here, the suffering all goes away. In the next moment, I'm off and running again in the world of delusion, struggling against what is. And then again I come back. That's what this practice is: finding the willingness to come back again and again and again."

Other people asked questions, and Cheri answered. The tension dissipated. I looked around, and everything seemed pretty normal.

But I was shaken. I wondered if I actually had taken the flowers into her room after all and somehow blanked it out of my memory. No, that hadn't happened. Still, I was seriously unnerved. To myself I said, "I am afraid."

It was the same kind of anxiety I'd felt on our previous visit to the rafting center. Once again, the room was threatening to close in on me. Fearing that I might faint or be sick if I stayed any longer, I rose, made a slight bow, and left the hall.

I walked to the restaurant, got a drink of water, went to the telephone booth, and called Sidney collect. When he answered, my tension was released in a flood of incoherence. I had come within a hairbreadth of making Cheri really mad at me, I said. And she had already been mad at me once. But it wasn't my fault, it was all her . . . unless maybe it was my projection.

Sidney's voice was soothing, but it was hard for me to concentrate on exactly what he was saying—something about the short path, about teachers who lead you straight up the face of the cliff. I said I was alarmed by Cheri sometimes. She could be so unpredictable, so unreasonable.

"Yeah, well, with some teachers," Sidney said, "all you can do is love them."

From the phone booth, I saw the group leave the workshop. Cheri was headed in my direction. There was a spring in her step, and she stopped for a moment to look up at the night sky. Clearly, she had let go.

But I needed more time before I could feel at ease with her. I thanked Sidney for listening to me, slipped out of the phone booth, and walked to the footbridge. I sat there in the dark for a long time, pondering what he had said.

Love her? When she acted so outrageously, when she upset me so? But, amazingly, when I considered it, loving her seemed just as possible as being upset.

Then a strange idea took hold of me—not one you encounter in Buddhism—that Cheri sacrificed herself for my salvation. Not in a personal or intentional way, but rather in the process of teaching and simply being who she is, she offers herself up, in some sense, precisely so that I might be *enabled* to love her. She lays herself open for the express purpose of giving me an opportunity for compassion. By letting go egocentricity's need to maintain identity as a spiritual teacher or an authority or a strong person or even a reasonable person, by giving up being right, being nice, she helps us learn to love ourselves exactly as we are and thereby love the world. All of her is right there, for better or worse; nothing is left outside, beyond the reach of compassion. Before our eyes, she demonstrates the practice she teaches: she becomes the unacceptable parts of me, and the compassionate awareness that embraces them. She is everything I fear, as well as the courage to face fear.

No soft, placid, meltingly sweet Buddha, this teacher, but one of those many-armed wrathful deities, fiercely wielding broom, scrub brush, frying pan, hammer and saw, ready to sweep out, wash away, sear, smash, slice, or otherwise demolish the armor of ego. The path she shows us is indeed straight up the face of the cliff, but she is right there with us every inch of the way. She will push, pull, exhort, cajole, resort to trickery, and even issue warnings—threats, almost—about time being short. And she will also wait in patience, in the calm certainty that there is an end to suffering.

I resigned myself to the likelihood that I would never know what was going on with Cheri. Once again, I was turned to myself, my own knowing. When I later told Cheri what I had gone through and my ideas about what it meant, she said simply, "Well, all you can know for sure is that that was your experience."

$$\diamond \quad \diamond \quad \diamond$$

On the morning of our last full day at the rafting center, Cheri had her kayaking lesson. For the afternoon, she had arranged a short raft ride down the river. She invited Joel to come over from Southern Dharma and persuaded me to join them.

Raul took a raft, paddles, waterproof suits, and life jackets in a truck and met the three of us at a point far enough upriver to make a short trip back to the center. Raul would steer the raft; the rest of us were to paddle forward when he told us to. Just before the restaurant, Raul said, we would hit the real excitement of the run, the rapids we had watched other people coming through.

As we were about to climb into the raft, Cheri asked Raul which seat offered the most exciting ride. The front, right up in the bow, could be plenty scary, he said. She turned to Joel and me, her eyes bright with anticipation.

"May I?"

We nodded, and she stepped into the bow and sat down.

A photographer stationed on the footbridge takes pictures of each raft as it plunges through the rapids. Whenever I look at my copy of the big color photo, I have to laugh. At that moment of intense awareness, each of our faces bore a telling expression. Raul looks in control, focused, his paddle backed firmly against the rush of whitewater, the tip of his tongue protruding, pointing in the direction he is steering the raft. Joel smiles a soft smile, his eyes looking upward, his paddle resting out of the water, going with the flow, as it were. I grip my paddle tightly, my face strained with the futile effort to avoid showing any apprehension. In the front, Cheri leans far forward, almost rising from her seat, her eyes and mouth open wide, stretching her paddle in front of the raft to meet the churning foam.

✧ ✧ ✧

It was twilight when Cheri and I headed back to the cabin. We stopped on the footbridge and sat with our legs dangling over the river. All the way up the walls of the gorge, fireflies sparked like tiny phosphorescent flares, silent explosions against the dark. Great bullfrogs raised their dark chant.

California doesn't have fireflies, and, seeing them for the first time, Cheri was entranced. Maybe, I thought, we are through with Sturm und Drang for a while. Maybe we can just sit here peacefully and enjoy all this. I let out a sigh of relief.

Cheri asked if I remembered our talking about lust, as I had called it. She wanted to point out the importance of not turning away from feelings. What you learn on this path, she said again, is to follow your heart.

I still wasn't sure what she was getting at.

It means staying open, even to things you're ambivalent about, or afraid of, she said. It means not denying yourself opportunities, of whatever sort, including relationships with people. "Because this is how we get to know ourselves, to see how we work. We'll never be free as long as we avoid things, as long as there are certain areas in which we can't trust ourselves." She went on to say that when she asked me about my experience of being strongly drawn to somebody, it was for her own reasons.

My mind grew agitated. In an attempt to steady it, I fixed my eyes on a rock in the river below, straining to anchor my attention to one spot in the turbulent water.

Cheri said, "I wanted to know how you handled that desire, because there is a similar situation in my life."

She was asking *me*.

"You mean . . . ? Oh. The person you've been talking to on the phone?"

She said nothing, which I took to mean "yes." My image of spiritual teacher as celibate monk, shunning attractions of the flesh—an ideal I had not realized I held—suddenly seemed naive and anachronistic. And yet there it was: the assumption that spiritual teachers weren't supposed to succumb to desire, anger, confusion, all those all-too-human traits.

"But isn't that kind of attraction just ego? Or . . ." I faltered.

"Well, you know, I'm not in this business because I have no experience of ego," Cheri said in a wry tone. "My qualifications are simply that I am willing to look at it very closely."

I took a deep breath and tried to settle down enough to observe my feelings. Anger, and under that, fear. It took patience, but I sat there and waited to see what was upsetting me. Finally, the words came.

"I am afraid for you to do anything that will bring you down from that pedestal where we put teachers. If you are too human, I imagine you can no longer be a teacher. I am afraid of losing you. I want you to stay a teacher for me."

Inside I was shaking at the thought of not having her in the teacher role. Yet, at the same time, another part of me was unmoved, knowing I would be all right.

She said nothing. We sat quietly.

The protection of the student role had been gently withdrawn from my grasp. I was left with an absence of roles in which I could find teaching within myself, without turning that into a role. The two of us could simply be who we were, in a way that felt, paradoxically, nonpersonal.

As I lay in bed that night, it occurred to me that the whole conversation might have been aimed to show me something I needed to know, and yet my sense was that her question was entirely genuine. Perhaps both were true. Her interests and mine, far from being mutually exclusive, may be intertwined, so that what serves her purposes also serves mine.

The next morning, we took cups of steaming tea out to the porch swing. A few drops of rain fell. We drank our tea in silence.

A pickup truck rolled up the gravel road and stopped. Two teenaged boys got out. One climbed into the back of the truck and lifted two lawnmowers down to the other. I watched them intently. Then I heard myself speaking, words for Cheri, for myself, for everybody. "I understand that living by rules is not freedom, and that denying yourself is no answer."

Cheri put down her cup. She looked at me, waiting for me to continue.

Heedless of the soft sprinkling of rain, the boys started their lawnmowers and set off on parallel tracks into the broad, grassy area in front of the cabin.

I heard myself again. "But what I hope for you is this: that however you act in this situation in your life, you will be able to feel the love that is already yours, to know the sufficiency of that."

As the lawnmowers neared the porch, their roar filled the air.

Cheri tapped my arm, put her hands together and bowed, mouthing the words, *Thank you.*

The mowers turned, and the drone receded.

Thank you. The words went to my heart, yet somehow they seemed to come from myself. The openness in my chest gaped wide. Once again, I felt totally exposed and profoundly safe.

Then I was struck with astonishment. "What I just said . . . it's for me. It's the thing *I* most need to know, for myself."

I looked at her to see if I was making clear this thing I could not explain. "I'm really telling this to myself," I said again.

"Yes," she said. "I understand."

Tears ran down my face, and the words kept coming. "So the thanking should come from me, the gratitude should—"

"Either way. Both ways."

"I should thank *you*."

"Whomever."

CHAPTER 16

THE GOOD MEDITATOR

JUST SIT STILL, AND KNOW THE JOY OF BEING ALIVE.

The next April, I went back to Southern Dharma for Cheri's annual visit. Spring arrived gently—each day a little warmer, the cherry and dogwood and apple trees progressing gradually from bare to blossoming—with none of the unseasonable surprises of the previous year. On the porch of the meditation hall, I saw that the wasps, whose nests had been removed once again to provide human visitors with an illusion of security, were steadily rebuilding. I admired their persistence, as I admired the steadfastness of the bird nesting under the low eaves, who, this year, kept her seat as I walked by.

The biggest change was that Joel had left. It was hard to think of Southern Dharma without him. His devotion to spiritual life, the openness with which he shared what he had learned along the way, had, for me, been part of the place. His absence was yet another teaching: he seemed to live, as they say in Zen, without leaving traces.

Joel's successor, Stella, on the other hand, had already made her mark, in a style more suggestive of resort than retreat. In the common rooms, posters and puffy cushions softened the spaces. Ivy and philodendron cascaded from the windowsills, and African violets shared a table with schedules, brochures, and the donation box. *The French Chef* and *The Silver Palate* took their places among the hard-core health-food cookbooks. Stella's liberality extended to spiritual traditions: on top of the library shelves, a framed sepia visage of Jesus faced a matching portrait of the Hindu master Yogananda.

I met Stella the same way I had met Cheri, in the kitchen. Stella too was wearing blue quilted footgear, the high-tech version, though: down booties.

"They're fantastic. You never have to have cold feet again," Stella asserted.

What about monastic austerity? I wondered briefly, then remembered Cheri's favorite dictum. *You don't have to suffer. It's not a requirement.*

Stella seemed to have attained considerable illumination on that point. Exuding a hearty hedonism, she looked glamorous and worldly, with cunning eyes and a wide smile. She wore shiny red lipstick and enormous earrings and leotards with matching skirts (one was a tiger-skin print, against which the blue booties struck a particularly incongruous note). Her hair, which managed to sustain a dramatic asymmetry, was white for an inch next to the scalp, then a mixture of black and an unnatural copper color. Having abruptly left a high-pressure, high-paying job to come to Southern Dharma, she explained, certain lifestyle changes were lagging behind. A year before, while reading Yogananda's autobiography, Stella had had a stunning revelation of ultimate purpose and devoted herself on the spot to serving God. It was just a matter of finding where to serve. When the manager's position opened at Southern Dharma, she took it.

Her first goal, Stella told me, was to liven up the retreat menus. Flipping through the recipe folder, she read off samples from Joel's repertoire.

"Wheatberry loaf. Squash and lentil pie. Miso soup and rice cakes." She raised an elegant eyebrow. "This idea that there's some contradiction between spiritual practice and eating well is the kind of thing that gives meditation a bad name. I'm giving them lasagna and garlic bread and dark chocolate fudge brownies."

Cheri liked the new food policy and the principle behind it. At the beginning of the retreat, she announced that if anyone needed anything to make themselves more comfortable, just ask Stella. I am witnessing the rapid erosion of macho Zen, I said to myself.

✧   ✧   ✧

Cheri brought good news. Her Zen group in California had purchased land for a monastery, and three people were living there as monks. Roy had turned up. Nobody knew how he had found the place without calling ahead, but there he was. He stayed for several weeks and made himself useful in getting the first construction project underway. Then he abruptly disappeared. Cheri was vague about what happened next, but it sounded to me as if she somehow had tracked him down in New Orleans and talked him into coming back to the monastery. The big red car had driven up just as she was leaving to come to our retreat.

I was overjoyed at Roy's return, and I could see that for all her discretion, Cheri was too. We hugged each other, held each other, blinked back tears. I felt as if I were on a team in which one member had been injured and taken away but had been miraculously recovered and returned to his place among us, inspiring us to play our game with greater dedication, greater belief in ourselves, so that we actually *became* better.

"I feel as if we've *won*," I declared to Cheri.

"Yes. Yes, I know." She nodded and beamed. "But look. We don't want to get too exuberant right now, because people are arriving for this retreat, and soon we'll be in silence. I know you'd like to run and jump and shout, and frankly, so would I. But I've got things to attend to. I've got a suggestion. Go sit. Let it all happen inside you. See what that's like."

We bowed, and I went straight to the meditation hall. Removing my shoes before entering the hall, I noticed that I did it carefully, in the most literal sense of the word.

❖ ❖ ❖

The retreat began with Cheri giving an explicit instruction: pay attention to where your attention is. The very idea produced a sickening sensation of tightness in my brain, deflating my buoyant mood over the news about Roy and the modicum of confidence it had produced.

Sitting was hell. I signed up in the first time slot for a guidance interview. Trying to pay attention to attention was making meditation impossible, I told Cheri. I couldn't do it. I was going nuts.

"All right," Cheri said. "Stop thinking about attention. Drop the whole thing. Just sit there. Hold the posture, and just sit."

"Just . . . ?"

"Just sit!"

I returned to the meditation hall and just sat. The thought arose, you mean it's all right to just sit here? I don't have to try so hard? You mean everything is all right just as it is?

When I realized, yet again, but in a much deeper way, that the answer is *yes*, always and unequivocally *yes*, my heart filled with sorrow, stretching back, it seemed, to before the beginning of beginningless time. Tears freckled the front of my shirt, and soon a great wet spot darkened over my chest. All this time everything had been all right? All my effort to change things, control them, fix them up—an illusion? All that was ignorance, unnecessary, self-created suffering?

Yes. I can just sit here. Nothing terrible will happen. I don't have to try. Just sit. Here, now.

I'm not alone. All these others are sitting with me. All others everywhere, we have all suffered the same misunderstanding. We fail to see the fundamental truth: everything is all right as it is. Including suffering. Because there *is* nothing other than what is. This is it. We miss it because we are not paying attention. We miss the glorious miracle, the unutterable beauty of it all. I cried for everybody who ever existed, for all that we have missed.

When, after four sittings, the thoughts and emotions subsided, I just sat. In the easy monotony of it, in the absence, suddenly, of anything more compelling to do, I watched my breathing. My attention would drift, and I would notice afterward what sort of thought or feeling took it away. Then I would return to the breath, but with an interest in seeing what would happen next. Something would capture my attention again, something kept dragging me away from myself, from the present, from the sufficiency of just sitting. Judgment (I'm doing it wrong). Fear (what if I stop thinking and lose control?). Distraction (I'd rather think about what I'll do tomorrow). On and on, the myriad varieties of unwillingness to be with what is happening. Like an endless succession of waves breaking on the shore, thought upon thought pulled me back into the cold, dark ocean of suffering. Here comes another one (daydreaming again, not really meditating), and another one (lay off, quit judging), and another (I'm sick of this). This is what I'm up against. But now, for the first time, I've got a foothold, I can stand fast, and the waves can come and go. I don't have to get washed away every time. And the breath can be the background against which I watch all the distractions that take me away from just sitting.

In the discussion that night, Cheri talked again about willingness. Until you reach the point of sitting every day with no struggle, she said, at least you could stop beating yourself up over it.

"One guy I work with beat himself up for years over meditation. He came to me in agony because he could not make himself meditate. I told him to throw away his cushion. 'Just throw it away. Take it to the nearest garbage dump and toss it.' He was so horrified that he walked out. In a month, he came back and reported that he had not missed a day of sitting since our conversation."

I anticipated the end of the story, and I recognized that the same stratagem had been used on me. With Cheri's exasperated *Just sit!*, I had been tricked into paying attention. If this were a religion in which kissing the hem of a teacher's garment were encouraged, I would surely have flung myself at her feet at that moment. I just laughed, and she just smiled.

The next afternoon, I walked in a light rain to the site where Anna's house had burned. It was almost covered over with vines and weeds. I looked down into the tangle of stalks and branches drooping with moisture. Dead vegetation from winter was dark and damp, halfway to compost, feeding the furry new leaves and buds, the whole woven into a little world of exquisite beauty. Solomon in his glory was no more splendidly arrayed—and this is what I miss when I am not present. What I watch for in meditation practice, I reminded myself, is everything that stands between me and this joy.

You can't do something to get joy, Cheri liked to say. *Joy is what's there when you stop doing everything else.*

✧ ✧ ✧

Over the next few years, I settled into a reasonably contented life with a good man, work I loved, a house and yard, pets and perennials and a slightly better car: all the things that Jane, my Buddhist therapist, had recommended for me. The wound of having been rejected by her healed into a scar that I hardly noticed any longer. One day I woke up and said to myself, "If I'm hopelessly neurotic, so be it. Life goes on. This is what I have to work with. And maybe Cheri's right—there's nothing wrong after all." Judging from the results, my being pushed out of the therapeutic nest was inspired tough-love wisdom. After all, one item that was not on Jane's list of things I needed was a therapist for life. At the top of her list, implicitly, was the dharma, and to the degree that Jane's actions helped me pursue that, I am grateful.

Cheri occasionally mentioned a ceremony for students who wished to acknowledge their commitment to dharma practice by accepting the Buddhist precepts. The precepts sound much like the Ten Commandments but are taken not as rules but moral guidelines to help deepen practice. When Cheri announced that she would offer a precepts retreat at Southern Dharma the following fall, I asked if it would be open to people who were not accepting the precepts as vows. She said it would. In that case, I said, I would be there.

Driving once again into the cove at Southern Dharma felt like coming home. The October day was warm, bright, clear, on its way to turning golden. The old apple trees were heavy with fruit, streaked dark brown and dull red among the gray-green leaves, beyond beautiful. Apples that had fallen on the ground were turning to cider and vinegar; the air carried a sweet-sharp pungent promise.

The retreat was to be ten days of meditation and discussion, at the end of which those who wished would formally accept the Buddhist precepts. Cheri had brought along a senior monk, Mark, to assist in the ceremony. It was his first venture out into the world after five years in the monastery they had built in California.

It was a soft retreat. Much of each day was given to discussions of the precepts, and the scheduled periods for meditation and working were balanced by liberal amounts of free time for reflection. Sitting on the cushion went as usual; I daydreamed, occasionally remembering to come back to the breath, but only briefly before I was off again. I recalled how at a previous retreat I had used my breath as a ground against which to notice what drew my attention away; I recalled "just sitting" and other insights and ostensible advances. But that was then, and this was now.

For individual guidance, I signed up with Mark, suspecting that Cheri had heard all too much about my identity as the Bad Meditator, whereas Mark was a fresh audience.

"Other people talk about expanded attention and observing thoughts and awareness of mind, body, and feelings, and I feel terrible that I don't have those experiences," I complained to him.

Mark responded as earnestly as if he were saying the words for the very first time. "Just keep coming back to the present. Do you hear sounds in the room? Feel the temperature of the air? Sense the presence of others? Isn't that enough?"

As he spoke, I thought to myself, yes, it is enough, and I do know that; I do experience the simple coming back from whatever draws me away from the present. But what draws me away is so powerful, so persistent, I told him, and so is the idea that I'm just no good at this.

"Still, it's important to treasure your practice," Mark said, "whatever it's like." He paused. "No matter how puny and pathetic."

Once I got over the shock, I had to laugh, and so did Mark.

Somehow Mark's words penetrated my fortress of resistance. He was turning my attention to the need for acceptance in an area I simply had not considered: my own spiritual practice. As I thought about that, I recognized within me two voices, one of someone who just doesn't want to meditate and another, faint but clear, of someone who—remarkably—does want to. I wrote a note to Cheri describing my discovery, and the next day I signed up for guidance with her.

When I entered, she beamed, "Well, hello, Good Meditator."

I burst into tears.

She handed me a Kleenex and said softly, "Who do you think has been bringing you to retreats all these years, if not the Good Meditator?"

✧ ✧ ✧

The first precept we addressed was "not to lead a harmful life," often written as "not to kill." I hadn't given much thought to the vows as such, which I considered beside the point, but I had imagined myself focusing intently on the discussions, incorporating each precept into my consciousness, and being magically transformed into a good person. The first morning, however, my mind wandered wildly, and I was less concerned with nonharmfulness than with what my work assignment would be.

At the end of the first session, Mark handed out slips of paper with handwritten job descriptions. I read mine: cleaning the skylight windows in the third-floor loft. How could it be that year after year, retreat after retreat, I was always assigned the job I most wanted? When I considered what it might mean, all I could come up with was that it was *all right* to have what you wanted—a notion stranger by far than unquestioned resignation to suffering.

I was standing on a stepladder in the loft, leaning half outside the middle window, lost in admiring the sweetness of the air, the dappled hillside across the cove, crisp leaves floating past, one blowing inside—when a wispy insect was smeared into nothingness by my paper towel. This on the day we considered not killing. But, as Mark and Cheri said, if we pay attention, we see how we break precepts all the time. Then we have the opportunity to extend compassion to ourselves in that very human situation.

During the retreat, I had a dream about moving into a different house. I had chosen the house, but somewhat reluctantly, because it did not match my idea of the kind of house I really wanted. And yet as I looked around when I was moving in, it turned out to be not only adequate but also wonderful in ways that surprised and delighted me. In addition to a vegetable garden, there were fruit trees and an herb bed that I hadn't noticed. The pantry, I discovered, was filled with canned garden produce. Five cats already living there readily made friends with my two cats. The house was more comfortable and more interesting than anything I had ever expected for myself, and more suited to me and my life than anything I ever had imagined.

At one sitting, I dropped into a relaxed state of easy, open, deep awareness in which I observed my breathing as a sensuous experience, observed my body sitting there in its profound sufficiency, even observed my mind, with its thoughts passing through, as wholly satisfactory. The world around me was mine, and yet "I" was just another creature in it. There was all the time in the world, for time extended infinitely in each moment.

In the past, I had often delayed as long as possible before heading to the meditation hall for each sitting, then arrived out of breath from dashing up the hill when I feared I would be the last person in. Now I was arriving at the hall early, staying late, even going up to sit during free time. Before, I had often looked for excuses to skip out of the walking meditations; now I was eager to practice maintaining awareness as I walked slowly, carefully, barely moving around the room. While I had previously envied or resented or dismissed the dedication of those who sat extra hours (the history professor who meditated in a down jacket with the hood up, wrapped in a Mexican blanket, continuing to sit every night when most of us filed out of the hall) and those who walked with total inward concentration (the kayaker who undertook each step with such deliberation, forcing the people behind him to adopt his frozen pace)—now I too had become one of the long-sitters and slow-walkers.

At last, I felt, I had entered into meditation practice. As if she had read my mind, Cheri concluded the nightly discussion by saying, "The teacher's job is to pull the rug out from under you, again and again, to force you to greater awareness. Whatever attainment you think you have, your understanding will always be changing. There will be no answer, no system—only the process of returning in each moment to the present, through whatever happens. Most likely, you will go through stages of bewilderment and frustration and fear and despair. When you do, just remind yourself: 'I am a person who is on the path to awakening.'"

That evening Cheri asked those who wished to accept the precepts to formally write out that intention, sign their names, and place their statements in a basket in the dining room. I did not think of myself as Buddhist, and I did not think of Buddhism as a religion. The matter of accepting precepts raised questions that troubled me. I wanted to ask, "If I take the precepts, will it mean that I am a Buddhist?" At the very thought, though, I was so overcome with emotion that I knew I would sob if I tried to speak.

When everyone had left the meditation hall, I sat outside on the porch and abandoned myself to a strange, deep crying I had felt building up in me. How can my life have come to this? I wondered. Come to what? I didn't know. How can such goodness be available to me? What goodness? I didn't know.

Leaping around in my mind were excuses not to take the precepts. When I considered the possibility of its being a natural and positive step in my life or contemplated that mysterious sense of goodness, ego would throw up a screen of rationalization. I watched it happen, and I stood back from believing it.

The next day, when I described that process to Cheri, she pointed out that great goodness already existed in my life, and I knew it was true. As for fear of being identified with a religion, Cheri suggested that accepting the precepts would simply be an acknowledgment of what was already the case: I had a spiritual practice, and it was Buddhist.

I don't remember actually making a decision or writing out my intention. What I remember is finally allowing myself the comfort of having something of my own, something to cherish and nurture, something to love and be loved by.

The precepts ceremony was characteristically Zen in its silence and simplicity, shot through with moments of high humor and deep paradox. I feared it might be like other formal initiations I'd experienced, from Brownie Scouts to college sorority, and I dreaded a replay of what happened on those occasions. The high-flown language and noble ideas had meant nothing to me, and I hated my falseness in pretending they did.

The very idea of formality repelled me. Would I have to offer incense? Recite strange words? Perform prostrations? Wasn't the ordinary good enough, especially in Buddhism? But I also knew that even if I felt unmoved by the ceremony, even if I thought it was ridiculous, I would live through it, and I would go right on practicing the path, just as I had for almost six years.

In fact, the ceremonies themselves turned out to be teachings, crystallizations of dharma. Since those of us accepting the precepts for the first time knew nothing about what the ceremonies entailed, there was nothing to do but be there and let it all unfold. Yes, just like life. Each moment resonated with its own quality; each moment was its own surprise. And within that, the big surprise was how utterly *true* it all felt, how everything we saw and heard and said and did was imbued with heartbreaking beauty, how the whole thing was simply about goodness. And how those three things are exactly the same.

Toward the end of the ceremony, Cheri committed herself to serving her students in their spiritual journeys. It made me think of Kabir's lines:

> The Guru comes, and bows down before the disciple:
> This is the greatest of wonders.

✧　✧　✧

After the retreat, without people around, it was quieter than ever—still, but filled with birdsong and insect chant and the soft rush of air, flickering everywhere with life. Wasps worked diligently on the exposed flesh of apples lying broken in the road. In the garden, giant sunflowers bent to face the ground, and birds perched upside down under the leathery heads to peck out the last seeds. A centipede scurried past a praying mantis along the bottom of the gate. Three huge cinnamon-colored ladybugs stood watch on a rotting zucchini. A soporific bumblebee clung to a half-opened zinnia.

Finally, there was time, and I set off to the high meadows at the top of the mountain. Just beyond the turn in the rocky, rutted road where Southern Dharma passes out of sight, I met six cows. One was black and the others a warm, rusty brown with white faces. They were as startled as I was and stumbled into one another trying to turn around and head the other way. The road was so narrow, with steep slopes on either side, that I worried that the cows would precede me all the way to the top, which would be unpleasant for all of us. Four of them, though, turned onto a barely visible path leading into the woods. The other two, who had been leading, missed it but were afraid to head back toward me, even though I stopped to give them plenty of room. I waited. They looked around and eventually clambered straight down through the brush.

At the top, I felt restless. I sat for a while on the rim of the bald, then moved down into a hollow in the meadows, where a wizened old tree grew from a cleft in a mass of boulders. I lay on the rock under its dense fan of bare branches, wanting to fall asleep but strangely energized. When the sky clouded over and a few drops of rain fell, I headed back.

In the distance, a sudden burst of sunlight picked out an ancient leafless apple tree weighted with golden fruit. I wondered how I could have missed it, then a cloud covered the sun and the gold faded into gray. On the way down, the sun came out once again, firing to their true color a last scattering of rose and copper leaves along the road. Beyond, I saw the cows, slipping single file behind a line of tree trunks, camouflaged in the speckling of light and shade.

I walked up the stone steps to the meditation hall. How different it looked from ten days before, when the tangle of blackberry vines, still green, reached aggressively over the railing and onto the porch. Now the branches were shriveled and broken, and the rocky soil of the slope showed through the crumbling foliage. How different from yesterday, when the entrance was festooned with sweaters and scarves and caps on pegs above a row of sandals and running shoes. Sitting on the bench to unlace my shoes and looking out along the path, I could see changes even from that morning. The drizzle of rain had spangled the lichen-covered boulders with luminous yellow-green, but already they were turning back to gray-brown as the moisture evaporated.

The whole place lives and breathes and changes in this transience. The end of the road: from the outside world, a long drive up and over a mountain, through a sparsely settled valley, along a road turning from blacktop to gravel, past a couple of dilapidated farms, through a stream. Around two steep, sharp, hairpin curves, up the one-car-wide track through woods and boulders for another mile (a long mile the first time, in which it enters your mind that you are lost), to the top of a ridge. Down then, winding past the First Great Sign of Impermanence, the ruined log cabin, back and forth along the steep, wrinkled contour of the old mountainside, arriving finally in an open space, welcomed by signs of habitation—a garage with a battered orange truck and the blackened chimney of the burned-down house. Then the outbuildings and finally the new buildings, extending a silent welcome to those who come to look head-on at what is.

I went inside to sit.

In the luxury of solitude, I thought of all the people who had sat there, with all their dramas of suffering and joy, coming and going like the voices of our minds, which worry and fear and hate and yearn and agitate. And I saw the meditation hall as a living being, containing the action, watching it all unmoved, just sitting, breathing, still.

A rustling outside. Reluctantly, I went out onto the porch to see what it was.

Four of the cows drank from a puddle in the road, then ambled toward the main building. It seemed unlikely that they would do any harm, but to be on the safe side I stomped and yelled, "Go away!" They responded with typical bovine confusion, bolting in several directions, bumping into one another, rolling their eyes.

A crashing in the underbrush came from up the hill, and I turned to see the other two cows. They looked doubly distressed, at their separation from the herd and at my presence. I sat on the edge of the porch and kept still. The stragglers made their way down, and the herd was reunited. Together, the six munched their way along the tufts of grass at the edges of the road and slowly headed off.

Gentle spirits, drifting, in these ancient shapes, into our sphere, through a brief turbulence, and out again into timelessness.

I went back inside and stood for a few moments.

White walls, lustrous wood floor. The building stands still through all these passing phenomena. Shades covering the skylights now against the sun. Raindrops evaporating quickly from the glass. Dry leaves and an occasional branch blown onto the roof with hiss and a clatter and then off again, tumbling, eddying down the hillside and away.

Set high in the front wall, the round stained-glass window representing the eight-spoked wheel of the dharma. I remembered that when I first sat there, the sun had struck the wheel between 4:00 and 5:00 in the afternoon, sending a shaft of red, then a shaft of gold slowly through the room. Sitting in a pool of light is the kind of experience it is easy to get attached to.

The sun would strike at a different time now. When? I'd have to watch.

The cushions were still in place along the sides of the room. I sat down facing the wall.

EPILOGUE

No dramatic transformations resulted from my formally becoming Buddhist. My personality remains what it has always been, with many of my old habits stubbornly entrenched. I still count myself among the meditatively challenged. I read and hear about experiences I do not have. On the cushion, deep concentration eludes me, while restlessness exhibits remarkable constancy. There are times when I meditate regularly and times when I don't.

Finally I have been able to settle into living in one place, with approximately the same degree of constancy that I manage in sitting on the cushion. That is to say, I know how important both of those things are in my life, and so I have an unquestioned commitment to them—and I also experience times of restlessness. Along with being settled have come possessions and routine. To bring some of the blessings of silence into the ordinariness of domestic existence, to remind myself of the possibilities opened up by spiritual practice, I resurrected an old idea, a "sabbath." One day a week, I make no social engagements, unplug the telephone, do no work, and spend the day in meditation and quiet and simple pleasures like gardening and listening to music. Just as sitting meditation does, my sabbath reinforces the shift often called "detachment"—simply stepping away from the entanglements of my own mind, dropping the turmoil and confusion, resetting all systems to the present moment. And each shift in that direction strengthens my underlying faith that, whatever happens, I have that refuge: by turning to willingness, I can allow life to be what it is, and then there is nothing wrong. The process is like opening and passing through a series of doors, never knowing what lies beyond, only that refuge is always available, here, now, that I need never again turn away from my experience.

The more willing I am to look squarely at the hard things in my life, the more softness I find in myself. And even when I'm not willing, something still works within me. Gentleness, for example, seems to grow in my heart like a tree-of-paradise in a sidewalk crack. No matter how I neglect it, it persists, indomitable, nourished from a deep source I cannot see.

I have lost interest in getting Cheri to explain karma and other arcane concepts in Buddhism. "Sit enough, and you'll sit it all," she assures me. Those things may or may not come to me, and it doesn't matter. I have been able to lay down the great burden of needing to have answers to big questions. What takes the place of it, perhaps, are moments I might call earthshaking, except that so far in my experience, the quality is the opposite: profound stillness and completeness and safety. In the sustaining yet impersonal joy of simply being present to all that is, the questions do not arise.

The world is a mirror in which I see myself. If I keep looking, diligently cultivating that larger awareness, there are moments when the mirror is gone, and the world just is. The practice seems simpler all the time, to the point of obviousness, like coming home. *As soon as you reside fully in yourself*, the teacher says, *you have the whole world.*

IN SILENCE: PRACTICE

A pane of glass separates me from the world.

For most of my life, I was unaware of any separateness, much less of what caused it, although often I had the sense of there being something in my way, restricting my movement, boxing me in, creating problems, the feeling of something just not being right.

When I step back and look from a different angle, the glass works as a mirror, reflecting the world—or rather my idea of the world, which is to say, myself. I practice looking at those reflected images because that seems to be the only way to see through them, to understand their nature, and to see beyond.

From another angle, I see that the glass is smeared and crusted with dirt, old dirt, accumulated over a long, long time. Little by little, I am clearing small areas, the easy ones first. A woman's version of the Zen classic, polishing the mirror, this is housewife Zen: washing windows.

Through the clear spaces, I see fragments of a bright and free reality. It is no different from the life I already know; to my unending surprise, it is, in fact, identical to it. But seen through the clear glass, this very same life has nothing wrong with it. It is fine just as it is.

I treasure each of those glimpses. A boy making noise in the meditation hall is simply a boy making noise in the meditation hall. A monk puts his lips out to touch a swaying willow branch, standing still while it comes and goes, comes and goes. Life happening in the form of trees, wasps, sleet, touch, walking, thoughts, laughter. The humanness of the teacher, baffling, maddening, disappointing, endearing, enlightening, so precious and poignant. My own fear, and my willingness to admit to it. These are tiny openings into my heart and back again into the world. Everything is here and then gone; I am here, in the midst of it. When I am still, the world explodes around me in its infinite perfection.

As I work away at the window washing, the clear areas of glass get bigger, there are more of them, and the scene before me becomes more complete. The more I see, the more I want to clear away whatever obscures my view.

It goes a lot faster with somebody working on the other side. The teacher is there, scrubbing, it seems, more energetically than I am, and tapping her finger at spots and blurs I've missed and stubborn smudges I try to ignore. I am encouraged by her presence. She looks me in the eye with a steady clarity that is at once a challenge, a refuge, a blessing. Sometimes she seems not to see me. Sometimes, when she knows I'm staring at her, she ducks out of sight. Sometimes I look for her and see my own reflection.

One approach I've heard of is to break the glass and be done with it. Maybe a time will come when I want to do that—or when the teacher tricks me into it. But shattered glass still has to be cleaned up.

For now, I'm content just to scrub, patiently, systematically clearing ever larger areas. Then I'll see. For now, this is where I take refuge, in the practice itself.